AMAZON FOR CMOS

HOW BRANDS CAN ACHIEVE SUCCESS IN THE NEW AMAZON ECONOMY

KIRI MASTERS

MARK POWER

Amazon For CMOs was developed with Laura Gale of Gale Creative. For more information, please see:

www.lauraiswriting.com

CONTENTS

Introduction   v

1. Navigating The New Amazon Economy   1
2. Formulating A Winning Strategy   20
3. Strategic Frameworks For Success   40
4. The Two-Edged Sword: Threats & Challenges   56
5. Winning On Amazon: Outcomes & Goals   73
6. Organizational Design In An Amazon World   95
7. Pick Your People: Talent & Partners   110
8. Future Opportunities & Considerations   123
9. Next Steps   137

Notes   151
Acknowledgments   153
About The Authors   155

INTRODUCTION

Jeff Bezos founded Amazon in July of 1994 in Bellevue, Washington, and what started as an online retailer for physical books soon expanded into a marketplace for electronics, consumer goods, music and video. In 2005, Amazon launched Prime, a ground-breaking membership program that promised two-day delivery to anywhere in the United States. By 2015, Amazon had surpassed Walmart as America's most valuable retailer by market capitalization, and by 2018, Amazon Prime had over 100 million members.

Since Amazon's inception, Bezos and his team have been relentlessly competitive, innovative and agile. At the time of writing, they are the world's biggest e-commerce marketplace, voice-assistant provider, and cloud computing platform. They are the world's biggest Internet company, the second-largest employer in the United States, and the most valuable company on the planet.

In the last 25 years, Amazon has thrived, while in many cases, traditional retail has floundered. Brands of all sizes have struggled to keep up with the rapid pace of change that the Internet and technology have brought to consumer behavior. Companies that have been in business for decades are facing collapse as their customers demand convenience and immediacy, while young brands are mandated to differentiate themselves in a marketplace where a frictionless buying experience, same-day delivery and instant customer support are entry-level requirements.

Amazon has been the driving force in this shift in the retail landscape. It continues to shape the way consumers buy, how they choose the brands they engage with, and what they expect from the buying experience. It's imperative that brands of all sizes and categories have a robust plan to navigate this new Amazon economy, and that the entire organization understands and supports the strategy.

This book is designed to empower the decision-makers to approach this critical moment confidently. Our purpose is to share insights into the most effective strategies and frameworks we've seen over the past few years, as we've led Amazon-focused agencies supporting clients in dozens of categories. This is not a tactical guide—you won't learn which buttons to click, the right keywords to use or how to game any algorithms. You *will* learn how to develop the Amazon strategy that is right for your business, how other industry leaders are steering their companies through this transformation, and how you can position your organization to grow and thrive in this new Amazon economy. We interviewed executives from companies all over the country, in both e-commerce and traditional retail, to share their strategies, to highlight the range of approaches that are available, and to create an opportunity for transparent, peer-based learning. Their willingness to 'pull back the curtain' on their brands' strategies paints a powerful portrait of the challenges and opportunities that many companies are exploring on Amazon.

It's also designed to provide senior marketing leaders and decision-makers with guidance on how to navigate the opportunities that will continue to emerge with Amazon into the future. The Amazon we see right now will likely be a completely different beast within the next few years. This book will empower you and your company to create an approach that sets you up for success over the long-term—even as the environment continues to change and evolve.

There are any number of books you can read about marketing, e-commerce and management. But we wrote this book because Amazon is entirely different to any channel that business leaders have dealt with before. We've structured the book around key Amazon leadership principles and frameworks like 'the flywheel' and 'Day One'—because part of developing an Amazon strategy is knowing how Amazon makes decisions and where its priorities lie.

We know all this because we've both been immersed in it every day for several years at our respective agencies. And because we come from completely different backgrounds, together we're uniquely positioned to help you understand the complete ecosystem and navigate it effectively.

Kiri launched her agency, Bobsled Marketing, in 2015 to serve branded manufacturers across Amazon operations, brand protection, advertising, and organic marketing functions. Today Bobsled is a fully remote team of 25 Amazon experts that consumer brands rely on to triage Amazon's evolving policies, programs, and best practices. Kiri is the author of another, more tactical book about Amazon—*The Amazon Expansion Plan*—and writes a weekly column for *Forbes* about Amazon. She is also the host of the E-Commerce Braintrust Podcast, and is the founder of the Marketplace Institute, an education platform for brands who are looking to develop their internal Amazon capabilities and up-skill their team with fast access to legitimate expertise along the way.

And with over 20 years of leadership experience in the digital marketing space, Mark has a proven track record of delivering innovative marketing solutions and growth for brands globally. He has successfully built agencies across the digital spectrum, most recently at Interpublic Group (IPG), where he led IPG's Amazon Center Of Excellence, a strategic capability that encompassed Amazon experts across display, search, brand building, and marketplace development. Mark launched his agency, Podean, after identifying an opportunity to assist both endemic and non-endemic clients (i.e., digitally native or not) to leverage the entire customer journey across Amazon and go beyond basic performance advertising tactics. Podean provides end-to-end marketplace marketing strategy and activation services to brands across performance media, brand building, customer experience, innovation and more.

For the past few years, we've found that the most insightful conversations about how brands are adapting to Amazon's presence in the market are often happening at happy hour or over private lunches. While some companies have been very formal and strategic in their approach, many other executives are feeling their way towards a strategy by tapping into their peer networks. CMOs and other senior executives at companies of all kinds are trying to understand the best approach to media strategy, organizational structure and balancing different sales channels—but there's no credible resource to reliably learn the best way forward. This book is designed to fix that, and to empower the leaders and decision-makers within brands to make informed decisions that help their company be competitive and adaptive to the demands of today's retail environment.

In the last fifteen years, marketing has gone from being fairly straightforward and intuitive to being very scientific and complex. It is *so* complicated (indicated by the fact that we now rely on data scientists to help guide us through the marketing world), and there are too many platforms and too many functions for any one marketer to be specialized in all of it. Google and Facebook alone are such vast ecosystems that they both require real specialization, and Amazon is no different. It requires complete immersion and constant attention due to its many moving parts and the pace at which it evolves. Very few marketers will ever be completely proficient in driving an effective strategy across every platform, so the marketing leader needs to have experts in place to advise them. The role of the marketing leader is to direct those experts according to the brand's strategy, while also juggling the demands of managing their team, driving innovation and producing outcomes that keep stakeholders happy.

Why Amazon Is So Different

Before we really delve into how you can do all that, let's lay out some of the differentiators that separate Amazon from the other channels and platforms we've all dealt with before. Firstly, Amazon functions according to an extremely demanding set of leadership principles. We'll be exploring some of these principles and accompanying strategic frameworks throughout this book, but in order to thrive in the Amazon ecosystem, you must understand how its leadership thinks about customers, how they evaluate new initiatives and why their policies, programs and best practices change so frequently.

Secondly, and critically, another reason Amazon is so

different is its data. Amazon has more data about consumers than any other platform in history. Sabir Semerkant, Chief Strategy Officer at NaturesPlus, captured its power for us:

> "There is no platform that can match it—Google can't, Facebook can't—Amazon has 25 years of consumer purchase data. They know exactly how we buy. It's not like Nielsen data or survey data—it's totally detailed and accurate, they know what triggers affect your behavior, and they know exactly what happens when we buy."

Amazon knows our buying habits, our demographics, what cars we drive, what credit cards we use, whether we have children, when we move house, when we are in-market for a certain product. While Google knows a lot about our intent, and Facebook knows a lot about our interests, Amazon knows what we actually research and buy. And if you look at where Amazon is going in the future—into content, experiences, voice, AI, brick-and-mortar and more—every touchpoint we have with them is creating more data for them to work with. Their data is just as valuable as their technology and logistics infrastructure, if not more so.

Amazon's ability to 'close the loop' on advertising and media with that data is also a key differentiator. To be able to tie the money spent to real outcomes is a huge motivation for marketers—they want to know how much they're spending, what they're spending it on, and which parts of the spend are actually working.

Amazon has also created an unparalleled logistics and distribution infrastructure that brands can tap into at a moment's notice. Even if your brand is tiny—with no negotiating power to speak of, and none of the volume that has historically made global distribution defensible—you can now set up on the most robust distribution network in the world, often in a matter of hours. Fulfilment, logistics and distribution no longer require the strategic focus and huge capital outlay that were previously required, thanks to Amazon's relentless focus on creating a seamless and reliable customer experience.

Additionally, Amazon's scale is now much greater than most people realize. It touches so many parts of society and culture. While Google provides daily utility, it is purely technology—it gives us access to powerful services, supplemented by select devices. Facebook is also primarily software. But Amazon is much more than that. It is technology, software, hardware, logistics, content, experiences, infrastructure—and it's only getting bigger, disrupting established industries like we've never seen before.

The Amazon Imperative

Amazon is now a strategic imperative for brands, whether you are selling products on its marketplace or not. Many brands, particularly in consumer product goods, are seeing their online sales far outstrip any of their traditional retail channels, and as we've noted, Amazon is no longer just a sales platform.

The growth of e-commerce has been explosive, and it's imperative that endemic and non-endemic brands alike keep up with this evolution. Endemic brands are those who are already selling via Amazon—they are native to digital sales, either because they were established during the e-commerce boom, or adapted early compared to the rest of their industry. Non-endemics are the brands who were either established before e-commerce took off and have not incorporated Amazon into their online sales strategy yet, or brands whose products are not feasible to sell on Amazon (but who could still take advantage of Amazon's other capabilities). Companies in the financial services, automotive and travel sectors have been classified as non-endemics, but this may change in the future as Amazon moves into these industries.

Both endemic and non-endemic brands face challenges. Endemics must be structured to scale effectively with media, and to effectively manage and take advantage of the mass of opportunities on the platform. Non-endemics must plan for the new Amazon economy, and treat it as much more than just a place to buy and sell physical products. Both must recognize that Amazon is a huge influence on commerce, society and culture that's here to stay and must be taken seriously.

As a strategic imperative, then, brands need to recognize that Amazon is more than just a marketplace, but a vast set of opportunities that they can leverage across data, content, logistics and innovative consumer experiences. Many brands must become far more organized and strategic in how they are planning for success across Amazon, and they need to understand that it's now a multi-billion dollar advertising business that is rapidly gaining power. It continues to eat away at the other 'walled gardens' in the media space (Facebook and Google) because of its unparalleled data, global scale and sizeable share of consumers' hearts and wallets.

For many brands, the biggest challenge is shifting the mindset around treating Amazon exclusively as a distribution channel. We've heard many CMOs and senior executives say that since their brand doesn't sell on Amazon, it's not relevant to their business at all—"we have other priorities" is a common refrain. To be fair, it is understandable that organizations have struggled to prioritize it: Amazon is massively complex. Even if you *only* look at it as a distribution channel, it's complex. There are so many programs and systems, so many rules and silos to navigate—it's completely different to selling to a retailer where you sit down with a buyer every three months who tells you what they want to buy. There's not much hand-holding with Amazon, very little guidance, and unless you are a giant CPG company, you're not likely to receive much face time with anyone internal at Amazon.

But that doesn't change the fact that Amazon is here to stay, and that it's absolutely imperative for your brand to have a strategy for dealing with it even if you don't sell there. Regardless of your business or industry, the only Amazon strategy we don't recommend is having no Amazon strategy at all.

There are two key drivers behind this. First, if you think your brand is not on Amazon, think again. Third-party sellers have most likely added your products to the platform, taking advantage of arbitrage opportunities (like buying in bulk at Walmart and reselling on Amazon). That raises the question of how important it is to be able to control your product supply, and to control the message and image that's being spread publicly about your company.

If third-party sellers are posting low-quality images of your flagship items, writing inaccurate product descriptions, and providing poor service to your customers (who don't realize that they are not buying from the actual brand who creates the product), your brand equity is in jeopardy. Typical customers don't know what happens behind the scenes at Amazon, and don't know who is responding to them or fulfilling their order. They just think, *"Wow, these are terrible pictures of this product that's normally good quality"*, or *"This item turned up late and it's expired—I loved this brand but they're really letting their standards slip."*

The second driver of this strategic imperative is that Prime has totally shifted the paradigm of how people buy. It has made buying online so frictionless that consumers are abandoning the habits they've had for decades. The traditional model of selling exclusively to wholesalers or to selected retail partners is a thing of the past.

Over 50% of American households have an Amazon Prime account.[1] That is a stunning opportunity for brands— not just because of the unrivalled market penetration, but because Prime members are highly qualified prospects. They have proven interests, they tend to be more affluent, and they spend more on Amazon than non-Prime members. According to some research, "Amazon Prime membership is lowest among households that make less than $41,000 per year... Households that made more than $112,000 per year, on the other hand, are nearing saturation, with 82% in possession of Amazon Prime memberships."[2] It's becoming clear that Amazon's advantage is in its access to that enormous pool of customers, but it's also a marketing channel with a proven path to purchase.

Exploring The Full Potential

There's a lot of opportunity for brands who decide that they're going to cultivate a mindset of partnership with Amazon rather than taking an adversarial view. Amazon has been viewed negatively by some brands, particularly for competing in saturated categories, its ambivalence about brand protection, and for its negative impact on traditional retail. But in our view, traditional retail has not innovated and adapted to the new preferences of the modern consumer. This created space in the market for a company like Amazon to come along, and in the long run, we believe that Amazon is actually going to be great for retail—because improved retail technology and a renewed focus on customer experience is going to be good for everyone.

Amazon's impact on consumer behavior is massive and transformative, and it's going to encourage innovation in industries and companies that haven't evolved in decades. Those that don't embrace change will become irrelevant and ultimately unsustainable. We're now in an era where Amazon is a viable, appealing marketing channel, but some brands still ignore it or view it as an adversary rather than an opportunity. As we mentioned earlier, there is a spectrum here: some brands don't engage with Amazon but have a robust strategic approach to e-commerce. For others, avoiding Amazon means that they are unable to leverage a vast customer engagement opportunity (considering that about 50% of all e-commerce transactions take place on Amazon's US marketplace alone[3]). If you think of Amazon as a partner, rather than a competitor or as a mere sales channel, your teams will be able to start exploring how to leverage the many opportunities that Amazon presents.

Forward-thinking CMOs are realizing what a huge opportunity Amazon presents for their brand. They are starting to pay close attention to how Amazon fits into their overall marketing strategy and media mix, instead of leaving it to the e-commerce or channel marketing teams to manage. They're now integrating Amazon strategies and tactics into their broader marketing activities, steadily growing in knowledge and skills around Amazon's marketplace and powerful advertising platforms. This in turn allows them to leverage the wealth of data available on consumer buying intent and habits.

The customer is Amazon's obsession. Their stated aim is to be the most customer-centric company in the world, and everything they do is filtered through this lens. It's one of their driving principles, along with another concept they call Day One: they treat every single day as if the company were brand new, and as if every member of the team were on Day One of a new role. Day One is shorthand for bringing your full attention and energy to the work, rooting out complacency, and being proactive in implementing new ideas and initiatives. Jeff Bezos said in a presentation that "Day Two is stasis. Followed by irrelevance. Followed by excruciating, painful decline. Followed by death. And that is why it is always Day One."[4] These leadership principles and frameworks are the foundation upon which Amazon is built, and are the road map to understanding how Amazon's business operates and evolves. Such insights can lead brands to possibilities far beyond just selling products or running ads. Kimberley Sweet Gardiner, CMO at Mitsubishi Motors North America, put it like this:

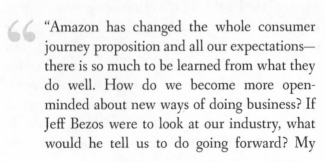

"Amazon has changed the whole consumer journey proposition and all our expectations—there is so much to be learned from what they do well. How do we become more open-minded about new ways of doing business? If Jeff Bezos were to look at our industry, what would he tell us to do going forward? My guess is that he would not do many of the things that we have been doing. It's time for us to make a leap, to think like Amazon does. They would be much more supply-chain focused, more focused on building efficiency into the system, removing waste from the system, and building innovation into our pipeline. Personally I want to think really, really big for this industry, not just for this company—how can we leverage the Amazon way of thinking about business problems, so that our partners and customers see that this is exciting?"

Kimberley's enthusiasm and sense of possibility is the perfect representation of Day One thinking. The automotive industry isn't even selling their core products on Amazon yet, due to regulatory restrictions, but she still sees just how much potential there is for growth and change as auto brands start to take full advantage of Amazon's capabilities. We invite you to read this book with a similar Day One frame of mind: open to discovering the possibilities Amazon could represent for your brand, curious about the impact you can have, and ready to take ownership of a transformative moment for your brand.

ONE

NAVIGATING THE NEW AMAZON ECONOMY

AMAZON HAS REDEFINED how we buy, sell and research. It has changed, forever, how brands and customers interact, and how brands need be structured themselves to thrive. It has created an entirely new environment, a new economy, to which we all must adapt.

Whether you currently look at Amazon as friend or foe, you need to get inside the mindset of Amazon's leadership to understand how they make decisions and how they look at the world, if you are to lead your brand to success.

This is why we will be infusing this book with Amazon's leadership principles, and the strategic frameworks that support them. Half the battle in this space is learning how to think like Amazon and trying to predict how the leadership will make decisions in the future—things change so quickly that this is one of the few constants we can rely on.

If you know how Amazon makes decisions, you can evaluate how they are likely to look at an opportunity and therefore how you can use that same opportunity to your own advantage. There are fourteen principles that direct everything Amazon does:

1. Customer Obsession

Leaders start with the customer and work backwards. They work vigorously to earn and keep customer trust. Although leaders pay attention to competitors, they obsess over customers.

2. Ownership

Leaders are owners. They think long-term and don't sacrifice long-term value for short-term results. They act on behalf of the entire company, beyond just their own team. They never say, "that's not my job."

3. Invent and Simplify

Leaders expect and require innovation and invention from their teams, and always find ways to simplify. They are externally aware, look for new ideas from everywhere, and are not limited by "not invented here." As we do new things, we accept that we may be misunderstood for long periods of time.

4. Are Right, A Lot

Leaders are right a lot. They have strong judgment and good instincts. They seek diverse perspectives and work to disconfirm their beliefs.

5. Learn and Be Curious

Leaders are never done learning and always seek to improve themselves. They are curious about new possibilities and act to explore them.

6. Hire and Develop the Best

Leaders raise the performance bar with every hire and promotion. They recognize exceptional talent, and willingly move them throughout the organization. Leaders develop leaders and take seriously their role in coaching others. We work on behalf of our people to invent mechanisms for development like Career Choice.

7. Insist on the Highest Standards

Leaders have relentlessly high standards—many people may think these standards are unreasonably high. Leaders are continually raising the bar and drive their teams to deliver high quality products, services, and processes. Leaders ensure that defects do not get sent down the line and that problems are fixed so they stay fixed.

8. Think Big

Thinking small is a self-fulfilling prophecy. Leaders create and communicate a bold direction that inspires results. They think differently and look around corners for ways to serve customers.

9. Bias for Action

Speed matters in business. Many decisions and actions are reversible and do not need extensive study. We value calculated risk taking.

10. Frugality

Accomplish more with less. Constraints breed resourcefulness, self-sufficiency, and invention. There are no extra points for growing headcount, budget size, or fixed expense.

11. Earn Trust

Leaders listen attentively, speak candidly, and treat others respectfully. They are vocally self-critical, even when doing so is awkward or embarrassing. Leaders do not believe their or their team's body odor smells of perfume. They benchmark themselves and their teams against the best.

12. Dive Deep

Leaders operate at all levels, stay connected to the details, audit frequently, and are skeptical when metrics and anecdote differ. No task is beneath them.

13. Have Backbone; Disagree and Commit

Leaders are obligated to respectfully challenge decisions when they disagree, even when doing so is uncomfortable or exhausting. Leaders have conviction and are tenacious. They do not compromise for the sake of social cohesion. Once a decision is determined, they commit wholly.

14. Deliver Results

Leaders focus on the key inputs for their business and deliver them with the right quality and in a timely fashion. Despite setbacks, they rise to the occasion and never settle.[1]

IN A POST ON LINKEDIN, David Anderson, Amazon's Director of Technology explained that while there aren't many things that are set in stone at Amazon, these leadership principles are the exception. They provide the essential foundation for every decision,[2] and while a lot of companies pay lip service to values and mission statements, Amazon's leadership principles are taken very, very seriously. These principles are in Amazon's DNA.

The company lives and dies by these fourteen points—they are totally ingrained in every aspect of the business. The leadership principles direct how they run their meetings, which candidates they hire, how they make their business development decisions and how they collaborate with external partners. It's why Amazon has been successful at a scale we've never seen before—these principles have been bred into the very fiber of the company and they have guided its growth with a very firm hand. This is how Amazon has developed itself so extensively—it keeps expanding into new spaces and keeps passing on that disciplined, focused profile, right from Day One of each new company's inception. The principles control every element of how the company develops.

Customer Obsession

Amazon's mission is to be Earth's most customer-centric company. The whole psyche of their business is about delighting their customers and making the entire consumer experience easy. It's an obsession, which means that customers gravitate more and more towards Amazon, because they have such good experiences there. In turn, this creates an upward cycle in brand affinity. In 2018, Bezos put it like this:

> 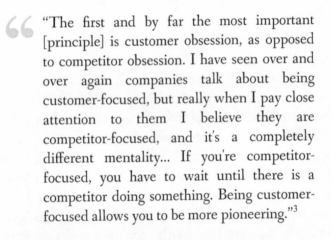 "The first and by far the most important [principle] is customer obsession, as opposed to competitor obsession. I have seen over and over again companies talk about being customer-focused, but really when I pay close attention to them I believe they are competitor-focused, and it's a completely different mentality... If you're competitor-focused, you have to wait until there is a competitor doing something. Being customer-focused allows you to be more pioneering."[3]

Amazon is now far more than just an online marketplace. Customers know it, and Amazon is capitalizing on all that brand value to continue expanding into new categories and industries. From a first principles standpoint, it makes sense—delight your customers and they'll come back again and again. This makes sense for any company, but Amazon has gone all-in on this approach. Amazon can launch new offerings and businesses in just about any area, relying on the massive bank of trust and goodwill they've built up with their customers—because their customers have been delighted so often, and they know that when something does go wrong, it will be taken care of immediately.

This creates the basis of the flywheel concept (which we will explore in more depth shortly): if customers are happy, that's going to attract more brands and more merchants, which drives down prices. Happy customers are a major source of momentum that drives Amazon forward, and we can all learn from this—what should a company be if not customer-obsessed? The only other option is to be competitor-obsessed. That's why we see such innovation in many of their initiatives—their focus is in a completely different place to that of everyone else in the market. Amazon's customer obsession has generated ideas and initiatives that seem totally crazy and are totally before their time. While not every idea has worked, this obsessive customer-centricity has served them incredibly well.

Sabir Semarkant, the former Senior Vice President of E-Commerce at VaynerMedia and current Chief Strategy Officer at NaturesPlus, explained it like this:

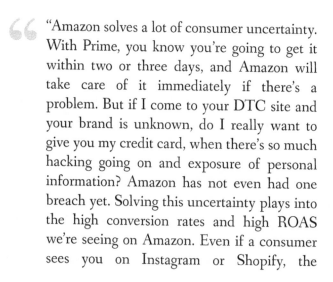

"Amazon solves a lot of consumer uncertainty. With Prime, you know you're going to get it within two or three days, and Amazon will take care of it immediately if there's a problem. But if I come to your DTC site and your brand is unknown, do I really want to give you my credit card, when there's so much hacking going on and exposure of personal information? Amazon has not even had one breach yet. Solving this uncertainty plays into the high conversion rates and high ROAS we're seeing on Amazon. Even if a consumer sees you on Instagram or Shopify, the conversion often happens indirectly on Amazon when the consumers searches the product name there—purchase consideration might happen on your DTC site, but the conversion happens on Amazon, because there's a lot of certainty there."

This is at the core of why CMOs really need to 'think like Amazon'—consumers are now expecting a Prime-esque degree of customer-centric service from all the brands they buy from. There is an expectation of convenience, immediacy, competitive pricing and ease, and they want it from everyone—from tech giants like Amazon, Uber, and AirBnb, to the scrappy DTC e-commerce brand, to the centuries-old, publicly listed national brand. We can no longer afford to think about how we differentiate ourselves with on-shelf or on-site offers alone. Brands need to deploy subscription-based models to meet customer expectations and build long-term customer loyalty; Amazon has trained the market to expect this. No consumer knew they wanted free, two-day shipping or an endless aisle before Amazon made it possible. But now that it *is* possible, brands need to update their customer loyalty models and start making aggressive moves towards identifying their own version of 'Prime', and ultimately serve customers to the same high standard that Amazon has done with this ground-breaking program.

The Consumer Transformation

Amazon's rapid expansion has not only transformed how brands sell, but how consumers buy. The customer journey (the experiences and decisions a customer goes through to make a buying decision) has evolved a lot since Amazon came on the scene. That's not slowing down, and is becoming more and more oriented towards Amazon and other platforms that give consumers the delightful and frictionless experience they want.

Customers go through a long process when they are deciding to buy a product, particularly when it's a first-time purchase, and will often assess a brand across multiple channels before making a decision. Amazon has assumed a critical position in that process: it's now where consumers go to verify the legitimacy and quality of the brands and products they are considering. Here's Christianne Pendarvis, the Senior Vice President of E-Commerce at plus-size apparel company Fullbeauty, talking about how their customer acquisition has been impacted by this shift in the consumer journey:

> "All shoppers look at Amazon as a search engine today. You must be there, even if you don't transact there or if only a small percentage of your transactions are there. At some point, a customer who starts in another part of your omni-channel ecosystem is going to look for you on Amazon to validate whether you're there or not. Unless you're a very big brand that she already trusts, that customer will devalue you if you are not there.
>
> With the data now available on Amazon, I can tell, for example, when a customer's first purchase happens on Amazon, if they repurchase on Amazon, if they used to purchase from us directly and then reactivate a year or two later on Amazon. So when I

> aggregate all those numbers, 85% of the sales
> are incremental—we wouldn't have gotten
> those sales if we had not been on Amazon."

IT WASN'T ALL that long ago that consumers didn't even have the option to research across channels. The only real channels available were TV, print, radio and outdoor, which were not interactive or targeted at all. Then along came the Internet, which gave us search engines, social media, comparison sites, e-commerce stores and an endless array of content to influence us. Amazon is currently at the apex of this transformation, with its endless aisle, programmatic marketing and robust review system. Amazon has recognized that channel switching is the new default human behavior and is giving customers exactly what they want on their path to purchase: transparency, control and convenience.

Consumers now navigate back and forth across multiple social media platforms, have in-store experiences, and use Amazon for both research and purchase. But Amazon also encompasses the customer journey when they're not even in the process of making a purchase. From watching Prime TV shows in the evening, to listening to Amazon Music during the day, to reading reviews about products—customers are constantly moving in and out of a purchasing journey, engaging with Amazon all the while.

Developing your Amazon strategy, then, is not about just getting better at the path to purchase on Amazon's platforms; we also need to consider the other experiential elements brands can provide for their customers so that they are constantly engaged, whether they are about to make a purchase or not.

In an email to subscribers in March 2019, Hilary Milnes, then the retail editor at *Digiday*, put it like this:

 "Being "channel agnostic" is the new "omni-channel." Retailers are recognizing not only do they have to be everywhere—with e-commerce, mobile commerce and in-store strategies—but they have to make it as easy as possible for customers to shop through any of those channels, regardless of whether it's less profitable for the company or a harder customer experience to figure out...

For example, at [retail conference] NRF, Kroger's CEO Rodney McMullen stressed that the future of grocery would entail meeting customers in multiple ways, depending on whatever is convenient for them at the time. One working mom might order online for delivery, pick up an online order in store, and shop at a physical location all in one week... "

This shift is also showing up in hard data, not just in reported behaviors. As Kiri wrote for *Forbes*, "a survey of 6,000 consumers conducted by Salesforce and Publicis.Sapient found that given a choice of retailers, brands and marketplaces like Amazon, consumers said they made 50% of first-time purchases from retailers, followed by marketplaces (31%) and brands themselves (19%). But when it came to repeat purchases, marketplaces won 47% of repeat purchases, followed by retailers (34%) and direct from brands (20%)."[4] The report went on to say that nearly a third of the consumers surveyed now preferred to begin their product research on Amazon.

This shift in consumer behavior is directly related to Amazon's place in the customer journey—it's closer to the point of purchase than Facebook and Instagram (which is good for initial product discovery and highly relevant recommendations) or Google (which is good for research). This brings us to advertising and why CMOs are shifting huge chunks of their media budget away from Facebook and Google, straight into Amazon's fast growing and maturing advertising platform.

The Amazon Advertising Opportunity

One of the biggest line items in the annual budget of most companies is marketing, and a massive part of that is media spend. CMOs are accountable for their media spend and have to justify to their CFO, CEO and boards that the marketing spend is being used efficiently and ultimately driving growth.

A major objective for the modern marketing organization is to allocate and optimize media spend across the multiple 'walled gardens'—Facebook, Google and Amazon—to deliver maximum return. Amazon is still relatively new as an advertising giant, and marketers are still analyzing what kind of budgets they should be looking to spend on Amazon. They also want to know what kind of return they can expect on that investment, and how that strategy is going to work with everything else they're doing. There has been a huge investment in time and money over the last ten years learning to make Google and Facebook advertising work for companies of all sizes, and now they've got another growing spend to control and integrate with the broader media mix.

Marketing decision-makers must determine how much spend to allocate to Amazon, which products to focus on promoting, how much they should be directing to test-and-learn budgets, and how to attribute success accurately. These are not easy questions to solve, because it's not in the interest of any of the walled gardens to solve them. If these attribution problems were made simple, advertisers would be able to see where their media spend is not optimized and immediately streamline to a more efficient approach, which of course, would mean less revenue for the advertising platforms.

This is where Amazon is starting to pull away from Facebook and Google—they are releasing new data sets and metrics that make it easier for marketers to attribute their spend more accurately, whilst building out a new marketing technology stack aimed at helping advertisers close the loop. Amazon's existing suite of advertising products are maturing and starting to become more integrated: its paid search product—Sponsored Ads—has delivered consistent ROI for brands who have consistently invested in the platform, whilst in comparison, advertising costs associated with incumbent platforms like Google and Facebook have risen rapidly and there is a less direct link to sales.

Nanigans, a performance marketing agency, surveyed 100 retail marketing executives, each responsible for $50 million or more in annual online sales. The survey found that by the end of 2018, Amazon was allocated 14% of this group's budgets (Facebook was allocated 19% and Google 21%), but more than 50 of these executives said they were planning to increase their spend on Amazon, either by shifting from Facebook and Google or by spending incremental ad budget there instead.

Data is the core reason for this shift. Advertising through Amazon gives brands access to rich data sets that no other platform can offer, and marketers are finding an edge with the precision targeting they can tap into with Amazon's extensive insights into its customers' buying behaviors and preferences. Additionally, because Amazon is a marketplace where sales occur, it can offer reporting and measurements that are more complete than the metrics that are available from Facebook and Google. These include ROAS (Return On Ad Spend, or how efficiently ad dollars translated into sales), ACoS (Advertising Cost of Sale), Brand Halo sales and other attribution metrics that help marketers understand what tactics are driving specific outcomes.

This is the ace card the other two giants just can't replicate: for brands selling on the marketplace, advertising on the platform can be directly linked to sales. Amazon knows every action the shopper took after seeing an ad (for example, clicking on the ad or adding to cart), and whether the shopper actually converted.

Amazon's reporting abilities aren't the only advantage here, either. While historically Amazon has been very conservative about sharing customer data, this is gradually changing. Amazon recently released a tool called 'Brand Analytics' for all sellers, which gives marketers access to key customer data, including customer demographics and analysis on what portion of sales were from 'new to brand' customers. These insights empower brands to tailor both their brand and performance campaigns to be more effective and efficient.

Attribution in advertising has been a challenge industry-wide for decades, and after many years of brands being frustrated by a lack of access, Amazon is gradually moving towards sharing more of this essential information. This shift is potentially a very powerful differentiator for Amazon's advertising platform. Pete Kim, founder and CEO of media consultancy MightyHive, explains the issue and how Amazon might pull ahead of the other walled gardens in the race for advertising dollars by giving access to this data:

 "Today, the attribution of advertising is 100% broken. One of the big industry secrets is that it always has been—there's never been a mathematically rigorous way to measure the very simple question of 'did I make money or not?' You've got reams of accountants who can tell you, down to the penny, exactly how much you spent and when you spent it. But if a CMO goes to their advertising partners and asks for estimates on how much revenue they drove, then adds up all the numbers given by those vendors, the total will inevitably be much greater than the total revenue of the company. So either the finance department lost all the money, or some of these estimates are wildly inflated.

And while Google is ahead on attribution right now, if you look long-term, Amazon has some amazing data points and assets that will help them a lot in this race. If you're going to do attribution—which is key, because then you can approve the marketing that is actually working—here's what you need: a data set of who saw which ad, a list of who bought what, and an identity graph that helps you bridge the two data sets. On one side, who saw what: you've got cookies, logins, and engagement. On the other side, who bought what: you have data like credit card swipes, email addresses, and mailing addresses. When these data sets are separate, the identity graph is the bridge that helps you connect these things, and Amazon doesn't just have an identity graph—they have a *mega* graph. They have more of that bridging data than anyone else, so they're pulling ahead in the race for attribution.

By definition, these data sets are big data, so it also helps to have the infrastructure beneath it all to support this process. Let's compare platforms: does Google have the who-saw-what data? Absolutely. Does Google have the identity graph? Absolutely. Does it have the infrastructure? Yes, it does. But it doesn't have the volume of *purchase* data. Same goes for Facebook. But Amazon has all of the fundamental ingredients for that recipe. They have the who-saw-what data, they've got the identity graph, they've got the purchase data, and with AWS, they've got the best infrastructure in the world."

And while the major motivations for advertising with Amazon are focused on the performance of the channel and ROI measurement, another powerful element is Amazon's audience. Its direct, advertising-driven relationship with over 100 million households through its Prime membership program which is an opportunity most brands just can't afford to ignore.

UNTIL RECENTLY, many marketers would have described Amazon's advertising products and consoles as immature and clunky, particularly when compared to Facebook and Google's intuitive and mature platforms. Amazon built its Sponsored Ads search product within its Vendor and Seller Central systems (which were primarily designed for brands and sellers to manage inventory and process orders from customers or wholesale purchase orders from Amazon). Squeezing an advertising tool into an already-extensive marketplace management console made it even more complex and resulted in a clunky user interface. Google and Facebook built their platforms the other way around, with their products being designed solely for the purpose of advertising (their core business). Their infrastructure is fully designed to build, deliver, optimize and report on campaigns, whereas advertising is still only one component of Amazon's overall offering.

Amazon first launched its paid search advertising product back in 2012, many years behind Google. This pay-per-click (PPC) advertising channel quickly became integral for brands to make their products visible and competitive in the marketplace, enabling them to advertise based on user intent (which is also how Google search became so successful). Marketers loved the sales-linked metrics that were produced, and advertising spend steadily increased. But the platform has still not matured to the standards that most marketers are used to, and still has some way to go. Amazon is yet to deliver the level of support, education or training that Google and Facebook have invested in, and it will take time for all of Amazon's products to be integrated into a single suite.

Until recently, Amazon's ad products have been less advanced in their capabilities—for example, retargeting and negative keywords were not available for a very long time. Marketers who have been targeting audiences through Google and Facebook for many years have recently seen increased pressure on campaign performance and increased costs to advertise, resulting in lower ROI. Amazon has not yet faced this downturn, and marketers have overlooked the shortcomings of their advertising suite in light of their ability to reach buyers with Amazon's incredible cache of purchasing data (and to do it in a cost efficient way—even if the brand doesn't sell products on Amazon).

While they're behind on providing marketers with an integrated advertising solution delivered through an intuitive user interface, we have to keep in mind that at the time of writing this book, only 2% of Amazon's revenue was related to advertising. Eighteen months before that, it was only 1%. This growth is all the more impressive since the leadership principle of frugality has meant that the Amazon Advertising Group has had major constraints on its progress and has had to split development resources across many projects.

Amazon has long understood that online advertising is highly lucrative, and that it is in a position to capture huge advertising spend and market share in the countries in which it operates. Despite this, the advertising platform has been a lower priority while the company focused on investing in other growth opportunities across the globe. However, in the second half of 2018, an Amazon insider confirmed that in an internal executive review meeting where Jeff Bezos was presented plans for all the major divisions, leadership from the Amazon Advertising Group were allowed two hours to discuss their plans—much more than the 20 minutes they usually receive. This would seem to indicate that the company will focus extensively on building their advertising business in the coming years.

Advertising is obviously a key element in this new Amazon economy, and one of the biggest challenges this presents to brands is that they don't own their customer relationship. All brands have to learn to partner effectively with Amazon, while developing their own relationships with their customers in parallel.

Historically, brands were all about customer relationship management—owning the data and nurturing the direct customer relationship. Marketing teams have typically utilized direct mail, direct response email, and other channels to drive visitors to their DTC sites and stores. But now brands are relying on third parties, so they don't always know who their customers are. This is also true of Facebook and Google and the other walled gardens that CMOs will need to navigate and plan for in the future (think AT&T, Verizon and Disney). This is the critical challenge, because it's difficult to formulate a winning strategy if you don't know exactly who your customers are.

But many brands have developed strategies that are allowing them to thrive in this new Amazon economy, and we've been fortunate enough to have many executives share their insights with us in the next chapter. Let's jump into the various approaches brands can take to creating the Amazon strategy that's right for them.

TWO

FORMULATING A WINNING STRATEGY

Amazon Leadership Principle: Ownership

"Leaders are owners. They think long-term and don't sacrifice long-term value for short-term results. They act on behalf of the entire company, beyond just their own team. They never say 'that's not my job.'"

WHEN IT COMES to developing the right strategy for your brand's engagement with Amazon, ownership is critical. The executive branch of the company obviously needs to take a firm lead on the strategy, but they also need to empower every person involved with Amazon across the company to take ownership too. This helps create a clear sense of cohesion within the organization and can generate the momentum and innovation necessary to thrive in this space.

Every brand, no matter how big or small, how

distributed or centralized, whether they sell online or not, *needs* a strategy for dealing with Amazon. We strongly believe that having a clear plan for partnering and interacting with Amazon is a strategic imperative for brands seeking success in the new Amazon economy.

The Strategy Continuum

There's a long continuum of strategies you can deploy here, but ignoring Amazon is not one of them. It is clearly not a perfect platform or perfect company, and it may not be the right sales channel for everyone. Regardless, even brands who aren't selling on the marketplace must have a strategy, because Amazon is expanding far beyond just e-commerce, and one way or another, its disruptive approach is going to impact companies across all industries. No matter the strategy you choose, consider how you will make your brand defensible and how you can leverage the many offerings across Amazon's vast ecosystem.

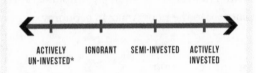

ACTIVELY   IGNORANT   SEMI-INVESTED   ACTIVELY
UN-INVESTED*   INVESTED

*with an actual defensible,
differentiated offering

The only part of this strategy continuum that you must avoid is 'ignorant'—ignoring Amazon or treating it as a nuisance that will go away. Unfortunately, some brands get stuck here. They are entrenched in old habits, or can't agree internally on their philosophy, so they never get started. Other brands aren't sufficiently differentiated from the market, and are not prepared to invest in reinventing themselves. Whatever the cause, ignoring Amazon often means that some or all of a brand's products end up being distributed by unauthorized third-party resellers. When a brand has no official presence on the platform, those listings (often with poor product photos, inaccurate content, and negative customer reviews) can start to erode brand trust on other channels.

Option 1: Actively Invested

One end of the spectrum of strategies is to be highly engaged on the platform. This means investing in Amazon's operational capabilities to leverage the full scope of the marketplace, marketing and advertising capabilities. It also requires shifting the mindset of the entire organization to view Amazon as a sales, distribution *and* marketing channel for the brand.

Going all in on Amazon doesn't mean that you stop selling through traditional retail or that you shut down your DTC site, but that you marshall all the resources of your organization and commit to making Amazon thrive as a channel. Here's how Sarah LaVallee, currently the Vice President of E-Commerce at Wandering Bear Coffee (and the former Director of E-Commerce at I and Love and You, a pet-care brand), describes the progression of getting an organization to go 'all in' on Amazon:

 "My first year at I and Love and You was spent rallying the organization, to prove the concept to everyone. It was getting marketing to create rich content, getting operations to look at e-commerce exclusive packaging options and so on. That first year we proved the concept by tinkering and getting the e-commerce and marketing basics correct, polishing our operations and making sure we were measuring the right things. By year two we had the board behind us, the organization behind us, so it was time to put on the gas.

If you're going to play on Amazon, you have to decide whether or not you're really going to go for it. If you're not going to go all in, you're really not taking advantage of all the great things Amazon has to offer.

We leaned in, and we started to see the business accelerate month over month. We had some great strategic vision for what we could do for the brand. We were up against some really big players, brands that were spending hundreds of thousands a month just on Amazon. We were small fish in the big sea, and yet we did so well that we became a truly insurgent brand.

Getting the strategy right meant we were able to take on incumbents that had huge teams of people to optimize absolutely everything, and by the end of year three, we were eating their lunch."

Another fantastic example of this 'all in' strategy comes from Anker, an electronics company who describe themselves as "charging experts and innovators of smart devices for entertainment, travel, and smart homes," who originally launched exclusively on Amazon. Despite starting out in an extremely competitive category (where Amazon has a private label brand), Anker has been wildly successful. They used Amazon as the unrivalled brand building platform it should be for so many companies.

Anker was started in 2011 by an ex-Google employee whose wife was selling products on Amazon. He built some software to help her be more efficient with that business, and her sales accelerated significantly. Seeing an opportunity, he decided to build an Amazon brand himself in the electronics space. Despite being such a saturated, competitive category, Anker built a very strong brand by engaging with the Amazon customer base to create genuinely innovative products.

When they started to get traction, the Anker headquarters moved from the USA to China, in order to be closer to their manufacturer. Using Amazon as a platform for testing ideas, they could get product feedback from customers, implement it with their manufacturers and have the updated products back out to the market in an incredibly tight timeframe.

Anker was exclusive to Amazon for several years, and they used Amazon's review mechanism as an integral feedback loop in their product development, branding and marketing. For example, if people were saying, *"I wish this cord was longer so my iPhone could reach my bed"*, Anker would take that into account and make products that would meet those customer desires. They built consumer feedback into their product development life cycle and, critically, into their content and branding as well. They really kept their ear to the ground—they started out just selling laptop batteries and chargers, but in responding to the market's demands, they've expanded their line to include all kinds of small electronic consumer electronics like headphones, chargers, storage devices and smart appliances.

Today, Anker products are sold in over thirty different countries. You can buy their products in Best Buy and Target and from their DTC sites. Anker developed in the opposite direction to most brands—graduating from Amazon to traditional retail—whereas most brands have been exclusive to traditional retail for a long time, and now they need to navigate Amazon in order to own their brand again and to be seen as relevant and legitimate by a new generation of consumers. This is an interesting brand building trend we're seeing, with Amazon-first brands embracing working backwards, and becoming very success-ful, legitimate stand-alone brands with this inverse model.

Option 2: Semi-Invested

Unless you have an offering that simply can't be replicated by Amazon, then your brand should be represented there in some way. Another model, shown in the diagram above as semi-invested, is halfway between the two ends of the continuum: we have both had clients who want to maintain a strong store distribution strategy (where they have existing relationships with major retailers or independent stores), but who also see the value in leveraging Amazon. These brands rightly see their retailer relationships as a defensible asset, and they recognize the value of enabling consumers to interact with their brand in physical locations.

For example, a footwear brand we've worked with knows that the 'try-on' experience in stores is critical for new customers, but they have also found that Amazon is a great platform for customers who may be ready to repur-chase. Those repeat customers already know their size and fit, so when they want to buy their second or third pair, they want to prioritize convenience, and go straight to Amazon.

Accounting for this shopper behavior means that the brand has now extended their customer experience onto Amazon. Instead of expecting customers to visit stores when they are already fans of the product, the brand invested in creating an Amazon storefront with high-quality product pages, and is running display media advertising to capture new audiences and build brand awareness on the platform.

This company's network of independent retailers are a

significant asset, and are critical in facilitating the customer's introduction to the brand and first try-on experience. Recognizing the value in these relationships, the brand allows a small number of independent stores to fulfil the orders that come through Amazon as third-party sellers, providing those stores with Amazon revenue.

This leaves the manufacturer in control of branding on Amazon, but not fulfilment, which is a healthy halfway point for their brand and its existing retail partners. You don't have to be all-in or all-out to find a strategy that will be successful for your company.

In another example of this 'Amazon-lite' strategy, jewelry company Charles & Colvard leverages Amazon's international sites to learn about consumer preferences in its different markets around the world. For example, they've found that shoppers in Spain prefer a more understated style of ring, compared with typical German shoppers. This then informs the inventory they feature and promote in each market.

CEO and President of Charles & Colvard, Suzanne Miglucci, says that her company uses Amazon as a channel to introduce customers to the brand and sell their most popular ready-to-ship items. But the brand also has a significant bridal business which requires a very broad range of style and customization options. This provides the best of both worlds—shoppers can find many core styles on Amazon and get acquainted with the brand, but will also shop directly on the Charles & Colvard website to order the majority of items.

Option 3: Actively Un-Invested

The other end of the continuum is where there is an active choice within the organization to have no involvement with Amazon at all. This is where we usually find brands who have already invested in their own fulfilment or logistics capabilities—often large retailers like Target or Walmart. This is also usually the choice for brands who have products which are either not allowed to be sold on the platform or are inherently unsuited to Amazon.

Some products are suited to this strategy because the gravitas of their brand prevents replication by third-party sellers or by Amazon themselves, such as luxury brands like Tiffany jewelry. This also applies to products that require a high level of personalization or customization, for which the brand engages directly with their consumer base.

For example, at-home hair coloring company Madison Reed produces hair coloring kits, which rely on specific information from the customer to select the correct color. This kind of experience, which promises customers they'll "find the perfect shade", can't be replicated on Amazon, because the platform doesn't support this type of personalization.

Another brand that relies on product personalization as a competitive moat is the supplement company Care/of. Co-founder Craig Elbert, previously Chief Marketing Officer of cult menswear brand Bonobos, told Kiri in an interview why he believes Care/of is still thriving without being on Amazon:

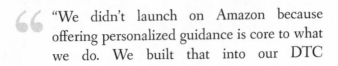

"We didn't launch on Amazon because offering personalized guidance is core to what we do. We built that into our DTC technology, and porting that technology over to Amazon would have been tricky or impossible.

Our product is ultimately a combination of digital and physical product, and that combination is part of the experience that we're delivering. If we delivered that directly on Amazon, it would have been a much lesser experience for the consumer, so in our case it was a conscious decision not to be on Amazon.

We do make our lives harder because we're not on Amazon and we're not in physical retail. 80 to 85% of purchases are still happening offline, and those that are happening online are obviously dominated by Amazon. So launching a brand outside both of those channels seems stupid at first, but it enforces constraints—you have to prove that you're good at storytelling, you have to prove you can build an audience, and that you can connect with consumers.

Over time as you prove those abilities and start to scale the business, you have more leverage in conversations with external parties —wholesalers, retail partners and so on. There's a lot of power when you have built up a highly desired brand on your own."

Like Care/of, some brands have a defensible position where they can elect not to be involved with Amazon as a sales platform at all (although that's not to say they couldn't make use of the other parts of Amazon's ecosystem).

In these cases, the defensible position is created by a

high degree of product personalization. In other cases, as with the new breed of 'digitally native, vertically integrated' brands, the differentiator often lies in the branding.

Take two cult brands, Away and Glossier, which operate in the luggage and cosmetics categories respectively: both have chosen to avoid Amazon. Both brands have achieved cult-like status through savvy brand marketing, and now have audiences who hang on their every word. Glossier founder Emily Weiss has said that "no woman has ever told me that their criteria for the best mascara was 'fastest' or 'cheapest'" (referring to Amazon's key differentiators), and that instead the brand relies on making an emotional connection with the customer. This position is something every CMO can aspire to, but cult brand status is rare, and very difficult to sustain.

Other brands test partnering with Amazon and then decide it's not the right strategy for them. For example, cleaning products company Truman's made a distribution deal with Amazon when the brand first launched. But Truman's said that since they were asked to give up so much data and direct feedback from customers, and faced such significant pricing pressures and distribution issues, that they decided to withdraw from the platform altogether.

Accelerating Growth With Amazon Advertising

Even for brands that have a defensible product and a moat between them and their competitors, Amazon's advertising platform is a huge opportunity to explore. Amazon's customers are a highly attractive demographic and can only be accessed by leveraging Amazon's advertising tools and consoles.

For non-endemic businesses—in areas like financial

services, automotive, travel and other products and services that can't (yet) be sold on the marketplace—its programmatic advertising platform is a powerful way to leverage Amazon's vast customer base and data sets. Amazon's DSP (Demand Side Platform) empowers advertisers to target unique audience segments with addressable display and video across Amazon-owned and operated properties, as well as Amazon Publisher Services, its third-party network of the top 400 publishers globally.

This access gives brands massive opportunities to reach a highly qualified audience, as well as the ability to target based on buying behaviors and preferences. General Motors has a presence on Amazon through Amazon Garage (as do Ford and most other big automotive companies), even though they're not selling cars on the marketplace yet. According to an internal source, GM spends over $30 million on Amazon each year for advertising and other auto-related initiatives. Auto brands are leveraging the data Amazon has on fifty million car owners to build their brands with display and video, and in turn, are driving new customers to brand experiences both inside and outside of Amazon.

Obviously, there's huge potential for brands of all kinds to use Amazon's data for marketing purposes. There's no denying that Facebook and Google have very powerful targeting capabilities based on intent, emotion, social connection, browsing behavior, demographics and various other methods of deploying their first-party data for targeting. But Amazon is unique in that it empowers brands to target based on actual consumer buying behavior—a completely new way to target customers with a proven interest in the brand or product.

Amazon is thinking far beyond advertising on their platform: it is facilitating connections and experiences between its customers and the brands themselves. It's new-age shopper marketing. Staying with the automotive example, Amazon has innovative solutions for the industry, even though the brands can't currently sell their core products on the platform.

First among these is the Prime Now Test Drive program, where car buyers can arrange a test drive with automotive brands like Hyundai and Volvo. The car is brought to the customer's home or office, at a time that's convenient for them to experience the car, and Amazon facilitates the entire transaction, reducing the friction in the lengthy (and often frustrating) process of purchasing a new vehicle.

Smart non-endemic brands are looking to Amazon's capabilities beyond just the e-commerce marketplace and advertising products, and see it as a vast source of highly engaged customers and a platform for innovation. Kimberley Sweet Gardiner, Chief Marketing Officer of Mitsubishi Motors North America, shared her view on this evolution in her industry:

 "There's so much opportunity to be had with Amazon that goes well beyond programmatic. The signals Amazon gets from customers who have had a transition in their life (maybe they've had a baby or started a new job) are so much more robust than any other media channel. I think Amazon has the ability to fundamentally, radically change the auto category and the entire path to purchase, how we go to market, how we listen to the signals that consumers are sending, and to do it in a way that feels completely intuitive. The beauty of Amazon is that it doesn't feel forced.

The potential is enormous over the entire customer journey; there's so much information and such a deep understanding of consumer behaviors and buying habits. Amazon's e-commerce framework is so robust —far better than anything else we're buying right now, in terms of in-market or near market environments—and the challenge is how to actualize that and to take full advantage of it. Really, programmatic and display are just table stakes in terms of tapping into the potency of how Amazon is changing retail."

Developing A Strategic Mindset

An important factor to keep in mind when you first start developing an Amazon strategy is to stay adaptable and to avoid becoming overly committed to a fixed strategy. This is because the Amazon environment is always changing. It requires an agile mindset—it doesn't work to pick a track and stick to it; this is a moment to implement 'test-and-learn' thinking across your organization.

The advertising world is constantly being surprised about new products Amazon is releasing and changes they're making to their platforms. Few people outside Amazon immediately understand what a new announcement will entail, or how to respond, so teams need to keep an open mind, stay adaptable and move fast. It's the same thing that happens when Google announces an algorithm update—there is always a huge ripple effect across all the companies and individuals who work with the platform.

It's key that you bring this expectation to building your strategy: that research is built into the process, that your teams are continually testing and learning what's working in their particular field (and reporting that to the other teams to ensure shared understanding and clear ownership of each element). It is highly beneficial to cultivate a curious environment across the teams and partners who touch your Amazon and e-commerce strategy.

This is also where we start seeing Amazon's leadership principles coming into play again. When it comes to building strategy, there are two key principles to keep in mind. The first is Think Big: *"Thinking small is a self-fulfilling prophecy. Leaders create and communicate a bold direction that inspires results. They think differently and look around corners for ways to serve customers."* The second is Bias for Action: *"Speed matters in business. Many decisions and actions are reversible and do not need extensive study. We value calculated risk taking."*

The key elements of your strategy, then, should include creativity, adaptability, curiosity, ownership, collaboration, and speed. We'll explore how to resource and lead your teams and partners effectively in later chapters, but first, let's look at some of the complexities that you will need to account for when you first start drawing a strategy together.

Creating A Holistic Strategy

Many CMOs run into problems as they start planning their Amazon strategy, because initially they think of it exclusively as a distribution channel. But if you treat Amazon like any other distribution channel, you will be stymied at every turn—both by teams with other priorities, and by Amazon's constant stream of new initiatives. It's far more effective to create a strategy that encompasses marketing, advertising, sales, product, operations, fulfilment and finance, right from the start.

Due to the impact on item-level profitability, a brand's Amazon strategy should not just be the responsibility of the e-commerce team. Senior leaders across marketing, product development, warehousing and fulfilment, finance, and the executive suite should influence and support the approach. It's helpful to think of Amazon as a business unit in its own right, that sits within your overall company. Michael Parness, the Chief Marketing Officer of the pet-care company Outward Hound describes Amazon as a micro-cosm of an entire business:

> "It's been such a difficult platform for many organizations to wrap their arms around because it spans operations, sales, marketing; it's a microcosm of everything that goes on in a business. So to hand it off to someone, like an e-commerce director, just doesn't work— it's not just one person's job. It truly is holistic account management at every level. It's about taking a 360-degree view of your whole business, through the lens of Amazon."

Amazon is a gigantic company, and whilst it is highly entrepreneurial, it is also extremely secretive about data and new initiatives. As such, it is siloed from an organizational perspective: the logistics arm of Amazon isn't involved in changes in marketplace seller recruitment, and the performance marketing teams don't have much exposure to what the advertising product division is up to.

There are very few people outside of Amazon's C-suite who really understand how every piece of the puzzle fits together, and that's why a lot of the discussions about navigating Amazon can feel disjointed. There are many different businesses operating under a single banner, and while they all have the same driving focus of customer obsession, they're each implementing that goal in a different way. It's impossible to keep track of how many different businesses are operating within Amazon, so your strategy needs to be able to adapt quickly in response to changes from all of them.

This is why it's critical to develop a holistic, cohesive strategy, and to ensure there is buy-in from everyone in the organization. You are going to need all hands on deck, all pulling in the same direction, to navigate the iceberg that is Amazon.

THE VISIBLE PART of the iceberg is what the customer sees. These things are relatively straightforward, tactical pieces—what your product page looks like, where your products show up in search rankings, where your paid ads are displayed. But out of sight, below the waterline, is a huge structure you need to pay very close attention to. These are the more operational elements that require a strategy to tie them together—the workflows, systems and people you will have to have in place to come out swinging on the platform, to protect your brand, and to start reaping the benefits of working with such a powerful channel.

Let's look at a specific example here: let's say, for example, that you don't have inventory available for a particular product that's usually available on Amazon. Without inventory available, Amazon won't allow that product to show up in organic search, and you won't be able to run paid search advertising for it either. That means that the workflows around inventory planning, forecasting and coordinating across teams are mission-critical. You can't have your content team running promotions to that product page, because all that traffic will be turned away empty-handed. Your media agency will be frustrated if they can't activate campaigns as planned. Finance will want to know why a rush shipment of inventory was authorized. Operations will get backed up and fulfilment across the board will be affected.

Above the water line, it looks like a minor irritation that a product is out of stock for a few days. Under the surface, it can be a massive setback to your brand's momentum on the channel (not to mention a major source of contention among your teams).

The iceberg concept goes some way to illustrating why it's not enough to treat content and advertising as a complete strategy. On their own, these are band-aid solutions for getting more sales—it's far more important to think about the whole channel in a holistic way. The platform was built with the intent that vendors prioritize operational factors, because ultimately, it's the operational factors that determine the customer experience.

Amazon's primary goal—to be Earth's most customer-centric company—drives every initiative and every new strategic play. When you're building an Amazon strategy, then, the most effective filter you can use for any decision is whether this strategy will delight the end customer. If it will, then the next filter is whether it will make Amazon money. If you can tick off those two requirements, you'll be in a good position.

Amazon takes these filters so seriously that it started building logistics companies to improve performance within their own business. Customer happiness reaches an all-time premium during the end-of-year holiday season, and Amazon knows that customers rely on the platform even more than usual for last-minute deliveries. At such a stressful time of year, peace of mind and a frictionless experience are never more valuable to consumers, but Amazon couldn't rely on the incumbent delivery services—UPS and FedEx—to deliver consistently during the holidays.

Amazon knew this was a customer delight issue, so they decided to build fulfilment options of their own. Now they have planes and fleets of tractor trailers, and they're funding all kinds of new initiatives to make their delivery systems even more robust. The only way to deliver every order to every customer on time is to have full control over the entire fulfilment and logistics solution.

There are dozens of Amazon-owned companies that don't make any business sense until you look at them through this lens of customer obsession—it's the only link and the only explanation for building such a disparate suite of businesses. Customer obsession is the glue that holds all the companies within Amazon together, and in turn, those companies add significant new revenue streams to Amazon's total business. Not every company can act immediately on the Day One principle, not every company can adhere to all the leadership principles—but every company can shift their obsession to delighting their customers.

THREE
STRATEGIC FRAMEWORKS FOR SUCCESS

Amazon Leadership Principle: Deliver Results

"Leaders focus on the key inputs for their business and deliver them with the right quality and in a timely fashion. Despite setbacks, they rise to the occasion and never settle."

———————

BUILDING A BUSINESS LIKE AMAZON—THAT has thrived beyond what anyone could have predicted—is only possible when the company is relentlessly driven by results.

The frameworks in this chapter have allowed Amazon's leadership to select the right inputs to generate massive growth, and to allow them to control the velocity and direction of that growth. Understanding these concepts will allow you to accelerate your brand's success on this channel.

These strategic frameworks also provide brands with the means of delighting customers and establishing a successful brand presence on Amazon's platform. These frameworks are the scaffolding built by the Amazon leadership principles, providing critical insights that should inform any strategic thinking about Amazon as a channel or opportunity for your organization.

The Amazon Flywheel

The flywheel is a popular growth strategy that has been used in business for many years, and Amazon has taken the concept to a whole new level. It demonstrates how they became so successful so quickly, and how other brands can become successful on the platform too.

A flywheel takes a lot of effort to start, but once it gets spinning, it gains momentum quickly and spins faster and faster.[1] This is similar to the snowball effect, where a snowball rolling down a hill gets bigger and faster until it comes to a stop at the bottom.

The difference is that unlike a snowball, a flywheel never has to stop, and Amazon's flywheel is showing no signs of slowing down.

Amazon has been very intentional about investing in the specific areas of its business that are essential to the flywheel strategy. Here is an illustration of Amazon's flywheel business model:

Amazon's early growth came from allowing third parties to sell on the marketplace. Sellers drive selection, so by having more sellers, you have more products in the marketplace. At the same time, having more sellers and more selection drives an efficient cost structure for Amazon, because they don't have to invest capital into infrastructure and inventory. Increased competition drives prices down, which attracts first-time customers. The greater the value and lower the price, the better the customer experience. Better customer experiences generate more organic traffic to the platform, and as the platform becomes more popular, it attracts more sellers, and more traffic, and the system gains more and more speed as it goes.

Then when you layer Amazon's advertising capabilities around the whole system, that starts to drive everything even faster: it brings more customers to the site, drives more sales, attracts more sellers, and a huge amount of revenue is generated as the cycle goes on and on.

From the very beginning of Amazon, Bezos and his colleagues have been focused on customer experience and low prices, to the extent that they've rolled out programs and products that can represent a significant loss to themselves. To compound the flywheel effect, Amazon's Prime membership, for example, provides plenty of perks, including friendly refund and return policies and incredibly fast deliveries to ensure shoppers keep coming back. The annual fee of Prime membership doesn't begin to cover the real costs that Amazon incurs in running it, but it promotes shopper loyalty and acts as a protective net around the flywheel.

Bezos has remarked in the past that one of the key reasons Amazon has done better than their peers in e-commerce is because they have been "focused like a laser" on customer experience, believing that this is critical in any business, but particularly online, where word-of-mouth is so powerful.

In order to initiate a successful flywheel for your own brand, you must ensure that each component of the flywheel feeds another. For instance, Amazon has excellent prices that lead to a high volume of website traffic. They offer free two-day shipping if you have a Prime membership, and once a membership is purchased, that customer will likely buy additional products to maximize their membership.

Advertising then drives additional purchases outside the Prime membership (such as the Amazon Echo and other Amazon devices, Amazon Music and Audible subscriptions) that add to the flywheel's momentum.

The flywheel strategy creates a cyclical pattern of success: Low prices lead to Prime membership, which leads to customer satisfaction, which leads to more sales and add-on purchases.

The reason we are exploring the flywheel in such depth is that too often, brands list their products on Amazon and expect to start generating a high volume of sales overnight. Unfortunately, it doesn't work like that. The flywheel takes some time to speed up, because there are many components that go into creating that momentum and consistent sales growth.

Andy Horrow, President of Protein2o (whose business was on track to grow by 150% on Amazon by the end of 2019) told us that understanding the flywheel is critical to early success on the platform. He said that generating momentum with your Amazon channel is a science that requires planning, patience and a careful focus on creating a great customer experience.

Unlike the direct response that can be achieved quickly from Facebook or Google marketing, growth on Amazon is much slower and much more involved. It's critical to factor this 'spinning up' into your timelines and allow a reasonable timeframe to get the flywheel spinning.

Winning The Buy Box

Another key element of an effective Amazon strategy is winning the Buy Box. Kiri explained this in her first book, *The Amazon Expansion Plan,* so we are reproducing that here to introduce you to this critical idea:

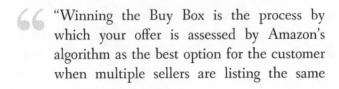

> "Winning the Buy Box is the process by which your offer is assessed by Amazon's algorithm as the best option for the customer when multiple sellers are listing the same

item. Winning the Buy Box is just Amazon's way of saying that you win the purchasing click from the customer.

So, no matter how many sellers are offering the same item, there will only be one listing for it on the Amazon marketplace. The seller who is currently winning the Buy Box, then, has *their* price displayed on the listing, so when a customer clicks 'Add to Cart', they get that particular price.

When there are multiple sellers of the same product, Amazon has to have a way to figure out who should get the sale. For example, if there are ten sellers of a product, and they all have different offers (such as different prices or fulfilment terms), who should win the sale?

To solve this, Amazon has their search algorithm that prioritizes relevance, sales velocity and conversion metrics, as well as comparing whether an offer is eligible for Prime (i.e. an FBA seller fulfilling through the Prime program, or Amazon themselves fulfilling through the Vendor program). Amazon will often win the sale if they have an offer on the product.

Another factor is price: the lowest priced offer will often win the sale, though not always. The other element that contributes to the algorithm is seller reputation—the length of time that seller has been active on Amazon, relative to competing sellers, and their overall feedback scores and success rates.

These are each of the factors that we currently understand as contributing to who wins the Buy Box. If other Sellers are selling your product, it's important that you give yourself the best chance of winning every sale.

You can do this by adjusting your prices, soliciting more positive seller feedback and customer reviews, and optimizing your fulfilment processes.

Now, while price is not the only factor, it *is* an important one. Seller tenure and reputation maintain and important role in the algorithm.

If Seller A has only been on Amazon for a few weeks, has only a handful of reviews and is offering a product at $30 (when Sellers B through F are selling it at $35), Seller A would probably still not win the Buy Box. If Seller A had been on Amazon for a few years, though, and had plenty of reviews, they most probably *would* win it."

In this diagram you can see all the inputs that influence the Buy Box product rank algorithm:

WITHIN MOST ORGANIZATIONS, Amazon falls into the remit of a single team, often the e-commerce or marketing team—but it's rare that the team in question is the only one actually interacting with Amazon, as we discuss in greater detail in Chapters 6 and 7.

When different divisions within a single company are not aligned, it can create significant issues around retaining the Buy Box. For example, being out of stock of an item due to poor inventory forecasting is a surefire way to lose the Buy Box. If your customer service team is letting shoppers down and eroding your seller feedback score, that can also contribute to you losing the Buy Box. And if your marketing team or e-commerce team is running campaigns that require you to be winning the Buy Box (i.e. any paid search advertising campaign), any gains they might make will be completely undercut if the national sales team is approving deals with retail partners who go on to sell that inventory on Amazon at a lower price than your brand does. This is how brands cannibalize their own progress—by not having a cohesive strategy where all divisions are working towards a singular goal under clear leadership.

For a brand to consistently win the Buy Box and grow sales, the whole organization needs to rally behind that goal. Difficult decisions may need to be made, such as which distributors, wholesalers, and partners can no longer sell the products on Amazon. It's very difficult to guarantee you'll win the Buy Box (or come as close to guaranteeing it as possible) when you don't have full control of your inventory.

Ryan Chen, the co-founder of Neuro, a nootropic gum company, explained his company's first-hand experience with this issue: after several press pieces started driving a high volume of organic traffic to Amazon instead of their DTC site, Neuro experimented with removing their brand from Amazon in order to realize more sales through their own website. They soon ran into issues with wholesale buyers who purchased inventory at wholesale pricing (around 40% off retail), with the agreement they would not resell that inventory on Amazon. However, several wholesalers broke the terms of their agreement and immediately started selling the products on Amazon. Chen says that trust with Amazon's customers is so critical that after just one month, Neuro returned to the platform to protect their brand equity. They regained control of the Buy Box and decided they had to own the channel and embrace the ecosystem of buyers who trust Amazon—even if it meant less traffic and direct sales on their own website.

Winning the Buy Box requires a very different mindset to the traditional approach of just selling as much inventory as possible on any channel. Prioritizing control of the Buy

Box requires investing in people, allocating the necessary resources, creating a marketing budget (including building the best possible customer experience on the platform), and critically, it also means potentially sacrificing sales from distributors and wholesalers with whom you might have long-standing relationships.

The impact of these decisions means that most brands need a senior executive, preferably at the C-suite level, to take ownership of this part of the strategy, in order to make bold, timely decisions about the company's actions on Amazon.

Far beyond just deciding if you should sell on Amazon, brands also face a paradigm-shifting decision here: whether you are going to persevere with the traditional whole-sale/distributor model that retail has used up until now, or if you're going to take the plunge and commit to making Amazon one of your primary distribution channels.

While many of the brands we work with have told us that while they had to make some short-term sacrifices, add more resources to get the Amazon flywheel running, and stand up to the demands of the process, this shift has been a very positive step into the future for their company.

Anticipate that retail partners who aren't part of the new strategy won't turn off an active sales channel like Amazon overnight, particularly when they still have an inventory position. Some retailers or distributors may continue selling your inventory on Amazon in protest, which can create channel conflict and brand protection problems.

Brands will need to take decisive action in this instance —Amazon refuses to get involved in disputes about distribution, so if you're going to pursue this type of action, the company needs to have a clear, aggressive stance. You may need to go as far as sending and acting on cease and desist letters; otherwise, the offending parties will continue to undercut your products, and other parties will see that the consequences are negligible and feel more confident doing it themselves.

Of course, many brands can't take an all-or-nothing approach and simply choose between Amazon and their other retail partners. One of our clients is a coffee company that couldn't control the fact that Costco sells their coffee in-store in pallets, at a discount the brand can't match on Amazon. Costco is worth up to $11 million in sales to the client annually, so it's not realistic to curtail that relationship.

This is where we come back to the strategy continuum —instead of owning Amazon as a brand-exclusive channel, the coffee company focused on minimizing the reach of other third parties that were competing with them on Amazon. They prioritized owning the Buy Box, and building their brand on the platform to make sure their marketing content and advertising was as sophisticated and thorough as possible. Ultimately, their growing business with Costco makes up for some loss of direct sales on the Amazon platform.

Sri Rajagopalan, former Vice President of E-Commerce at Johnson & Johnson, described that early in their e-commerce journey, Johnson & Johnson hadn't been successful in their Amazon strategy, and so they started over to find the right approach at a different point on the continuum. He shared his insights on the *Jason & Scot Show* podcast:

> "When I started, J&J had stopped shipping to Amazon. There were a lot of issues with

quality, and it was a mutual decision to stop that relationship. We were experimenting with DTC, so the goal was to start up all pieces of e-commerce—omni-channel, marketplaces and Amazon, B2B, our own DTC e-commerce, and we had to start it up from scratch. We had to put together a team and get going in all directions. We were fortunate that consumers have responded, retailers have partnered with us, but let me just put out some truth here: when it comes to e-commerce, you're not going to be able to do it all yourself. You're going to have to partner with vendors, and the more the better."[2]

The Shift From Third Parties to Brands

In order to get their flywheel going when first building the marketplace, Amazon had to focus on onboarding a large number of sellers who could expand the assortment, drive prices down, and start building momentum. But at a certain point, adding more sellers has a diminishing rate of return, and having more sellers can create more problems than it solves.

Amazon has since decided that it is more advantageous to shift their attention from third parties to brands, since brands will invest in R&D for new products, develop great content, and focus on building their relationships with consumers. For example, when Nike invests in creating high-quality Amazon product pages with videos, 360-degree images and detailed product information, the intent is that a customer will have a similar brand experience on Amazon as they would on Nike's own website, and this of course is a very different experience to what the customer would have with most third-party sellers.

When brands invest in creating great products based on strong market knowledge, then sell those products on Amazon, it creates more demand on the platform—more traffic, more selection, more purchases. Brands also care deeply about the customer experience, ensuring products are described accurately and arrive in good condition. That consistent, high-quality experience is more aligned with Amazon's customer-centric intent, and so they have started prioritizing brand direct relationships over resellers, whose main contribution to the Amazon ecosystem has been to deepen inventory positions and drive down prices.

To facilitate more brands launching on the platform, Amazon has rolled out tools and capabilities to brand owners that are not available to the reseller cohort. That includes Brand Registry, which proves you are the owner of the brand and allows you to create enhanced content on your product pages. Brand Registry also gives you access to specific types of paid advertising that are not available to non-brand registered sellers, and access to more analytics (including customer demographics and metrics like 'new to brand,' which shows how many of your customers bought from your brand for the first time in the last twelve months).

There is also the 'Transparency' program, which prevents sales of counterfeit inventory for enrolled brands via a barcoding system, along with Project Zero, a self-service counterfeit removal tool for sellers which Amazon says is "empowering brands to drive counterfeits to zero."[3]

This is why we are at such a powerful moment in time—there's never been so much scope for brand success on Amazon's platform. Brands have more power than ever over their presence on the platform, and can access insights and opportunities that are not available to resellers.

Operating At The Pace Of Amazon

While brands now have more tools and programs to leverage than ever, Amazon's platform is also uniquely demanding. The rules change often, and information is often siloed and sometimes contradictory. Amazon has many algorithms, which each determine an individual function, such as who wins the Buy Box, where a product displays in the organic search results, which pages will show your sponsored product ads, and where your display ads will be shown.

These algorithms continue to evolve, and brands need to understand that what might have worked for them a year ago in winning their Buy Box or ranking a product may change over time as Amazon finds better ways to display products and improve conversion rates. This is why an agile, flexible strategy that focuses on communication and collaboration is so critical.

Jon Regala, Head of Sales and Business Development at Sony Mobile, put it like this:

 "You have to move at the pace Amazon moves, and that means the pace of the digital space. Don't craft one thing and decide that's how it's always going to be. Don't treat it like we've treated traditional brick-and-mortar retail, where you plan something for months and then once you launch it, that's it. You've got to dive back in, look at the data, see if what you have is working, and be willing to quickly change that.

For example, if you put some messaging on a product page that you think should work, but don't see evidence within the first week to support that, take a shot at changing some of that content and see if it drives any of your key metrics more effectively. Be willing to change. Dive deep into their analytics and adjust as fast as you can read the data."

To take full advantage of the platform's scope, there needs to be a collaborative effort across the organization (and across divisions) to build your Amazon strategy and to navigate all these challenges. It can't be done in silos. It's critical to be proactive about accelerating and optimizing the areas that are working, and to be clear on how you're going to acknowledge and address the inevitable challenges that will arise.

Let's say the overarching decision is that your brand is going to control your end-to-end sales, logistics and supply chain on Amazon, with no third parties or other distributors. Leadership must all agree on the investment that will be required, and whoever leads this initiative needs to be empowered to have a clear mandate and the legal clout to make that happen.

Alternatively, the strategy might be to empower distributors to sell your products without degrading the brand quality on the platform. That's where the continuum idea comes into play again—instead of relinquishing all control to distributors, your brand might choose that semi-invested position, controlling all the content and customer experience, and making very clear agreements with all your distributors about the minimum pricing and conditions of sales.

Regardless, if the goal is to be in full control of your brand on Amazon, then, like we said, it's likely you will have to sacrifice some short-term revenue and be tough on distributors who are not acting in the brand's best long-term interests. Whatever you decide, it's key to determine what success looks like for your brand. Work backwards from that goal to identify all the necessary measures, and to ensure that all the involved parties in your business clearly understand the strategy right from the start.

FOUR

THE TWO-EDGED SWORD: THREATS & CHALLENGES

Amazon Leadership Principle:
Have Backbone: Disagree and Commit

"Leaders are obligated to respectfully challenge decisions when they disagree, even when doing so is uncomfortable or exhausting. Leaders have conviction and are tenacious. They do not compromise for the sake of social cohesion. Once a decision is determined, they commit wholly."

ESTABLISHING your brand on Amazon is a demanding task that requires sustained attention over time. Of course, the pay-off can be extraordinary, but most companies will face quite a few challenges along the way. In this section, we cover the most common issues that arise, so that you can be as prepared as possible.

These issues have kept many brands from getting involved with Amazon in the first place, or have stopped them from taking full advantage of the platform. Foremost among these are counterfeiting and unauthorized third-party sellers, Amazon's private label brands, policy issues and margin concerns.

Challenge #1: Counterfeits and Unauthorized Third-Party Sellers

Many companies have walked away from Amazon, or have avoided getting involved in the first place, as a result of Amazon's ambivalent attitude towards helping brands resolve disputes with counterfeiters and unauthorized sellers. JBL, a major electronics brand, refuses to sell on Amazon directly, because from their perspective, Amazon has refused to deal with the counterfeit issue. A source within the company said that JBL considers this such a serious breach of standards that they refuse to even advertise on Amazon. Though they've recently started to allow approved third-party sellers to sell on the platform—likely because the opportunity for sales on Amazon is just too powerful to ignore—from JBL's perspective, Amazon has historically been complicit in the sale of counterfeit products.

Complicit is a strong word, but it does sum up how many brands feel about Amazon—that Amazon is exclusively in it for their own gain, and that counterfeit products, fake reviews, disingenuous competitors and unauthorized sellers are just the cost of doing business within the Amazon ecosystem.

This seems counterintuitive if you go back to the first principle of customer obsession: allowing fly-by-night operators to sell suspect products is not very customer-centric. Customers hate getting counterfeit products—they feel misled by inaccurate or incomplete content, and are disappointed when they buy products based on five-star reviews that turn out to be fake. Counterfeit and unauthorized sales have created a lot of customer experience problems on the platform, which in the eyes of many brands are not being appropriately addressed.

Nike is another brand that did not sell directly on Amazon for a very long time, because Amazon wasn't controlling third-party resellers to the degree Nike expected. Courting Nike was the first (and to date only) time Amazon has agreed to assist a brand in maintaining their selling position (by blocking third-party resellers from competing for the Buy Box). However, that deal was struck about three years before the time of writing this book, and we are yet to see an appreciable reduction in the number of third-party sellers who are selling Nike products on the platform.

There's no specific policy from Amazon about protecting brands from unauthorized resellers. Even if you're a brand like Nike that procures a special deal to protect your brand, there doesn't seem to be any guarantee that it will be enforced, which means that it falls to your brand's legal department to manage any unauthorized activity. This is the essential tension here: the cost of defending your brand on Amazon can be astonishingly high if your product is easily counterfeited, or if it's available for purchase at a lower price through other channels.

Despite the extent of this problem, and all the costs associated with running an Amazon channel, some brands *still* find that all the trouble is worth it.

PopSockets (a brand that makes the little widgets you stick onto the back of your phone so you can hold it with just a couple of fingers), found themselves in this situation. They had a very public disagreement with Amazon about unauthorized sellers on the platform. After investing heavily in their Amazon sales and advertising, the company pulled out of selling on the marketplace altogether in late 2018, because Amazon wasn't taking appropriate action on unauthorized and counterfeit sales. *Digiday* reported on the suit PopSocket filed against Amazon and other marketplaces in early 2019:

> "PopSockets details the problems with unauthorized online sellers: It's impossible for PopSockets to control the quality of products sold online, the products don't come with warranties despite being advertised as such, and customers associate the defective products with the PopSockets brand, not the seller. Negative reviews have piled up on Amazon in response...
>
> [However] PopSockets are now available on Amazon again through authorized sellers. It speaks to Amazon's weight in the industry: Sitting out all together can hurt brands more. But its fight against fake products continues: CEO David Barnett has said that the company has spent $7 million defending its patent in the past year, and that seemingly "hundreds" of fake products pop up on Amazon and other marketplaces like eBay every day."[1]

There's also an argument that brands themselves are Amazon's customers, but Amazon really hasn't extended their definition of a 'customer' beyond the end consumer of each product.

This is one area we feel that Amazon is falling short of meeting that standard of customer obsession. It's disconcerting that many brands feel so badly affected by this issue that they are not even willing to advertise on the platform to take advantage of Amazon's unparalleled market penetration and data capabilities.

Challenge #2: Amazon's Private Label Brands

Often we'll hear concerns from brands that Amazon will expand into every category on the platform with their own private label or house brands. These companies are, understandably, concerned about bidding against Amazon on Amazon's platform. They don't like the idea that they've been investing so much in this channel and that Amazon has been utilizing all that data—all the analytics, sales trends, buyer behavior—to further their own plans to launch private label products. Since Amazon can use their own ad inventory as they please, brands are potentially competing against a player with almost unlimited advertising resources.

This is perceived as an unfair advantage for Amazon, since they can adapt their price points, fulfilment processes and advertising strategies, at almost a moment's notice. They can develop products at scale based on all the data they have about the product attributes customers want, the price points that are missing in a given assortment, and the search terms the market is using to find their desired products. (If this is ringing antitrust bells for you, we'll come to that later on.)

However, it seems unlikely to us that Amazon is going to invest extensively in the manufacturing game. Their private label brands are designed to fill gaps in the assortment that customers clearly want. In most categories, we see a premium national brand—say, Patagonia, producing their performance outerwear—which invests in supply chain innovation and R&D, designs ever-better products, and has powerful brand equity outside of Amazon that's been painstakingly built over many years across many channels.

Then at the other end of the category, we see no-name brands selling low-cost hiking jackets directly from the manufacturers in China. There's no brand equity, there's no proof of the quality, there's no inspiring content or brand building going on, so while it may be a perfectly fine product, there's a big question mark in the customer's mind about the quality of the product and the type of buying experience they're going to have.

The difference (in price and quality) between a $400 Patagonia jacket and a $40 no-name jacket is obviously enormous. And for the assortment to be complete, by Amazon's reasoning, there needs to be an option in the middle: a product that meets the needs of a customer who cares about quality but is also concerned about value, and who wants more assurance than buying direct from an unknown manufacturer but is indifferent about choosing brand-name items. That's where Amazon is coming in with its private labels.

Amazon is using its data to identify gaps in the assortment, supply chain, and customer experience, and developing brands and products that meet those specific value requirements. While it's not solely to the benefit of the customer—Amazon is clearly doing this to generate additional streams of revenue too—we don't think they're trying to kill established brands. Coming back to their customer obsession, it's more about identifying what creates a good customer experience, and identifying where they are missing items and opportunities to deliver a good product in a price range customers are looking for.

For an article she wrote for *Forbes*, Kiri spoke with Alexandre Manoukian, Head of E-Commerce at Nestlé Professional, the B2B division of the company. Manoukian believes that Amazon lacks the category-level expertise that would allow them to enter categories with private label brands and add any significant value to consumers beyond what is already present in the market, without destroying the overall value of that category.[2]

Amazon needs national brands as much as national brands need Amazon, due to the established credibility and reach of those brands (particularly in categories more nascent to e-commerce, like grocery and B2B). This relationship might explain why the vast majority of Amazon's private labels are concentrated in a handful of verticals and often in lower-priced categories:

> "Amazon's private label offering contains 6,825 products across over 100+ identified private labels. 4,674 of those private-label products are in apparel... 'Clothing, Shoes and Jewelry' take up three-quarters of all private-label products, followed by 'Home & Kitchen' and 'Tools & Home Improvement'... 40.5% of the total products are below $20. In the top four categories with the highest number of products, apparel and food items are mostly below $40."[3]

So while concerns about Amazon's private labels are fair, they're not cause for panic. However, there *is* another conversation that runs parallel to this issue: how brands can overcome complacency in a marketplace where they have been successful for a long time, and may have stopped innovating and building connections with customers.

The whole point of having a brand at all is to create a demarcation of quality—a statement about the lifestyle or values or benefits that matter to the customer. If Amazon is able to come along and undercut that product by $10 with their private label offer, and take away that market share, then what kind of brand does that business really have? Organizations that see this scenario as a real possibility have most likely not been diligent to stay defensible in this evolving marketplace environment.

Sri Rajogopalan, former Vice President of E-Commerce at Johnson & Johnson and now Senior Vice President of E-Commerce and Digital Sales at Revlon, shared his thoughts on Amazon private labels in an interview on the *Jason & Scot Show* podcast:

 "I don't worry about private labels at all. I think there are two pieces to this: private labels have existed for a few decades, this is nothing new. The industry is panicking a lot looking at Amazon's private labels, saying, *"this is going to do something to my brand equity."* My question to marketers is straightforward: if you've built brand equity over many years, and you're going to lose confidence over one announcement, are you sure you're doing the right thing? Brands will always have equity and Amazon's private label will also always be equity-based.

The second piece is that manufacturers haven't spent a lot of time looking at whether they should be partnering with retailers and developing private labels. I don't mean just manufacturing a product in a factory and putting it on a truck, but owning marketing elements around it, creating equity for the brand. With the experience manufacturers have, wouldn't retailers want to partner with them on the marketing part of it as well? I see it as awesome, it's an opportunity for every manufacturer to leverage. The good ones will figure it out."[4]

If you are genuinely investing in your brand, developing great products, building your customer relationships, they we really don't think you should worry about Amazon competing with you, because they're not doing any of the R&D or brand building that you are. So while the concern is valid if you don't have a defensible brand, it's overstated if you have been diligent about differentiation. Charlie Cole, the Global Chief E-Commerce Officer at Samsonite, told us in an interview that even established brands like Samsonite and Tumi cannot rest on their laurels in the new Amazon era:

 "As Amazon has grown and challenger brands have emerged, you start to get to the ultimate question every brand should be asking themselves: *why should a consumer buy your brand?* For us, durability is sacrosanct to our business, and our long-term presence in this market gives us an opportunity to engineer something better than everyone else on Earth. In a marketplace world, that's a hard story to tell, and I'm really proud of how we're adapting. We differentiate ourselves *after* the sale, by focusing on after-sale service and all the additional value we can provide to customers after they've bought something from us.

Amazon and other private label brands are not in the warranty and repair world, they're not in the lifetime value world, they're not into value-adds via loyalty programs. So focusing on how to drive a consumer relationship after the sale is one thing every brand and manufacturer should be talking about, because commoditized brands don't want to worry about that stuff, they're not in that business."

Challenge #3: Antitrust and Marketplace Diversification

As we were writing this book, we were asked several times if we think Amazon is vulnerable to antitrust regulation from the Federal Government of the United States. In short, we do. In an interview with *Marketplace Pulse*, antitrust expert Sally Hubbard explained that the current state of affairs—where Amazon is able to leverage its monopoly power to distort competition—is unsustainable and likely to be challenged extensively in the coming years.[5]

But even if Amazon is broken up, or forced to restructure, it's still going to be massively powerful. Antitrust concerns aren't a valid reason *not* to use the platform, but they *are* a reason to diversify your presence across multiple online marketplaces and to ensure that you have a clear overall e-commerce strategy in place for your brand.

At the time of writing, Amazon is the only platform that has made the kind of investment necessary to fully capitalize on the unstoppable growth of e-commerce. But players like Walmart, Kroger, and Target are starting to catch up, building marketplaces where brands can sell and participate in partnership programs. Those platforms are also developing advertising programs, and some are building their own fulfilment networks too.

However, many brands still need to define their own e-commerce objectives (including their DTC strategy), and should focus on resourcing and running their own e-commerce strategy smoothly, before worrying about tackling Amazon and all the other marketplaces. Once your brand's own online commerce capabilities are established and contributing to sales and revenue, you can prioritize bringing your Amazon presence up to speed, followed by other marketplaces as you choose to expand.

While there is a need for diversification across marketplaces, DTC brand building is also critical. If you don't build your own brand over the next few years, you're not going to be able to differentiate yourself from any of the marketplaces on price, delivery or customer experience. Your brand risks becoming completely commoditized, so having a long-term brand building strategy will provide the strong foundation you need to execute a robust e-commerce strategy.

Challenge #4: Margin Concerns

As we mentioned in Chapter 3 when talking about strategic planning, executives must be realistic about how long it will take to ramp up Amazon as a significant sales channel. There's a lot of investment required to get an Amazon channel up and running, and to get the flywheel really spinning with media and sales. The investment in time and money is substantial, especially in highly competitive categories, and this understandably gives many brands pause.

It's hard to specify the exact profit margins that brands can expect from Amazon, because it varies widely across categories and price points. On one hand, Amazon is a conversion machine. Every pixel on every site and app they own is optimized for conversions, and so the traffic that visits your Amazon product pages is likely to convert more than it would on other sites (including your own DTC site). Again, there's huge variation by category—you will see lower conversions on a pair of boutique jeans than you would on branded laundry detergent, and low price-point items convert higher than high price-point items. But in general, the traffic you send to Amazon is likely to convert at a higher rate since it's a reputable site and the preferred place to shop for many consumers.

Despite a strong conversion rate, many brands still find that it's more expensive to sell on Amazon from a margin standpoint. Eric Bandholz, founder and CEO of Beardbrand, said in an interview on the podcast *E-CommerceFuel* that the average order value (AOV) on their DTC site is $55, while on Amazon the AOV is only $25. This is due to the fact that Beardbrand can offer customers an up-sell or cross-sell on their DTC site, whereas on Amazon, products from other brands are often recommended. *E-Commerce Fuel's* 2019 "State of the Merchant" report confirmed that most small-to-medium sized brands have a similar experience to Beardbrand, with better margins on their own site than on Amazon.[6]

To stay competitive on Amazon, it's becoming more and more important to make your products Prime-eligible, particularly if every other brand in your category has done so. (And this is not just about organic sales—Prime eligibility impacts the search algorithm, which in turn affects the efficiency and performance of your advertising, which impacts brand awareness and top-of-funnel activity.)

Unfortunately, making products Prime-eligible comes at a cost, and this is where a lot of margin concerns are now focused. Prime requires brands to either use seller-fulfilled Prime or to send inventory to fulfilment centers, or for vendors, to ship orders directly to customers. These costs eat into the margin the brand receives from each sale, but the search and product ranking algorithm prefers Prime-eligible items, since shoppers will generally have a better experience if they purchase a Prime item.

This affects the search rank of the products, and if you're competing in the Buy Box with other sellers for a specific SKU, you're more likely to win if you're Prime-eligible (even if you don't have the lowest price).

So while it does reduce margins somewhat, we see such a profound difference in sales and conversions once a product becomes Prime-fulfilled that the volume of purchases can quickly eclipse any loss of margin (assuming that you are profitable on the sale of each product).

Challenge #5: Chasing A Moving Target

Amazon is famously (and frustratingly) opaque on their constant updates to policy and best practices. Rules, processes and algorithms are continually changing, and because Amazon is so siloed, it sometimes seems impossible to get a clear answer about what's going on. There are many grey areas that brands run into with Amazon's terms of service and their guidelines about using the platform, but there are two major issues that account for most of the problems brands experience when dealing with Amazon.

The first issue is the regulation of securing product reviews from shoppers. Many brands overestimate how important and powerful reviews are in the Amazon marketplace: how heavily reviews influence product rank in the search results is a big misconception.

The reason for the confusion around reviews is that in late 2016, Amazon changed their rules around marketplace sellers giving out free product to consumers in exchange for reviews. This was a very common practice (and companies were giving away product samples to generate word-of-mouth long before Amazon came along) but the activity had become so prevalent that Amazon felt it was distorting genuine customer reactions to products. So Amazon decided to regulate the practice extensively—disallowing brands to incentivize product reviews in any way, including giving away product samples in exchange for reviews.

This completely up-ended a key element of a significant marketing strategy for many brands on the platform. If a brand doesn't understand Amazon's strict updated rules in this area, they might be inclined to ask their staff for reviews, or their friends and family, or offer an incentive for a review, without realizing that Amazon views that as a major breach of policy. Brands that are caught incentivizing reviews are usually banned from the platform with very little recourse to have the account reinstated.

The second issue arises in assortment planning. Many brands would prefer to keep their bestselling items exclusively on their DTC e-commerce site, or in-store with their retail partners, leveraging Amazon to sell their slow-selling inventory (we'll tell you a cautionary tale about that shortly). These brands try to force customers to switch to DTC channels in order to purchase the most in-demand products, but this is not customer-centric and it almost always causes problems. It creates an opportunity for third-party sellers to put your popular products up for sale on Amazon, which often means that the brand loses control of the Buy Box and potentially causes brand protection issues.

Not only that, but it frustrates the customer—Amazon is often the channel they find most convenient, and it's where they've ordered this kind of product in the past. By forcing them to other channels, the brand is creating a negative customer experience, and possibly driving the shopper into the arms of competitors who have a substitute product available on the site.

Toys "R" Us: A Cautionary Tale

Amazon expects brands to be totally compliant with their policies (even though they change so often), and can become an implacable enemy, should you choose to make one of them. The conflict between Amazon and Toys "R" Us has become retail lore, but in the event you missed it, this is an important lesson about contravening Amazon's core tenet of customer obsession.

In 2000, when Amazon first wanted to get into the toy category (a huge strategic category for them), they approached Toys "R" Us with an exclusivity deal, where Toys "R" Us would have been the exclusive supplier of toys on the platform for ten years. Today, it's hard to imagine the incredible advantage that a single retailer would have if they were the exclusive supplier of a given category—especially for a period as long as ten years.

But Toys "R" Us—whether due to hubris, protectionism or a lack of imagination—did not list the inventory of their most popular products on Amazon. We assume this was because Toys "R" Us wanted to drive people back into their stores, or because they thought it would limit Amazon's expansion into the category, but whatever the reasoning, they did not make the most in-demand toys available on the platform.

Once Amazon recognized that Toys "R" Us was undermining Amazon's goal of providing a complete product selection, they sourced third-party sellers to fill out the gaps in the assortment, in spite of the exclusivity agreement. Toys "R" Us promptly sued Amazon for breach of contract. The two companies came to an undisclosed settlement, but the only explanation for Amazon's actions is that they took a calculated risk, knowing full well that Toys "R" Us would sue them. Evidently the value of having a full assortment of toys on the platform outweighed the cost of a potential settlement, and that pay-off was buttressed by the brand equity generated by keeping Amazon's customers happy and loyal.

We believe this story really comes down to Amazon's customer obsession—they were willing to face up to a lawsuit in order to get the selection their customers wanted and to continue building the momentum of their flywheel. By comparison, Toys "R" Us wasn't really interested in the customer experience—they were focused on driving customers back into their stores. Toys "R" Us refused to adapt to how people wanted to buy, and chose instead to try to force customers back into stores, which isn't how customers (time-poor parents) wanted to shop.

This story highlights the misstep that some brands make when designing their Amazon strategy: listing only a partial assortment of their inventory on the marketplace. The logic is that they will place some products on Amazon but reserve the post popular items for their e-commerce site or preferred retail channels. This is a false economy, because it's trying to force customers to transact outside of their preferred channel.

While you might make more margin on the sales from your owned channels, you're likely to generate fewer sales than you would on Amazon. If a new customer is searching for your flagship product on Amazon but is unable to find it there, they may not make the extra effort to seek it out elsewhere. And all the while, your competitors are waiting in the wings, bidding on that search term and picking up that demand. By forcing the shopper outside of Amazon, you might lose them altogether.

FIVE

WINNING ON AMAZON: OUTCOMES & GOALS

Amazon Leadership Principle: Invent and Simplify

"Leaders expect and require innovation and invention from their teams and always find ways to simplify. They are externally aware, look for new ideas from everywhere, and are not limited by 'not invented here.' As we do new things, we accept that we may be misunderstood for long periods of time."

AMAZON FOSTERS AN ENVIRONMENT WHERE INNOVATION, lateral thinking and massive ambition are rewarded. This encourages their teams to think big (another leadership principle), to take risks, and to push themselves to the edge of what seems possible. How can your team do the same?

When Amazon begins the process of developing a new product, program or feature, the executive in charge pitches the venture internally by writing up a mock press release announcing the finished product. If the team doesn't get excited when reading the mock press release, or don't think that customers will be excited, they often go back to the drawing board.

This is called 'working backwards', and it's another of the strategic frameworks around which Amazon operates. It prevents the company from developing products and features on an unfounded hope that customers will respond well; the entire focus is to ensure the project is something the customer will actually love.

They begin by asking themselves what the customer wants, how the customer will feel, and whether this product will improve the customer's experience. If the answers to these questions are positive, the project moves forward; if not, something significant will have to change before it's approved.

In a profile in *Business Insider*, the CEO of Amazon Web Services, Andy Jassy is quoted as saying:

> "Amazon uses this 'working backwards' approach because it forces the team to get the most difficult discussions out of the way early. They need to fully understand what the product's value proposition will be and how it will be pitched to customers. If the team can't come up with a compelling press release, the product probably isn't worth making. It also helps with more rapid iteration and keeps the team on track."[1]

There's no denying that this approach works. Stephanie Landy wrote a mock press release when she pitched

'Amazon Magic' to Jeff Bezos. Amazon Magic became Amazon Prime Now, a service that delivers household items, and other common products with free two-hour delivery. To date, this service is offered in several major cities across the globe, and accounted for almost $6.5 billion in revenue in 2017. Landy, now the Vice President of Amazon Prime Now, wrote the following mock press release for her pitch:

> "This morning Amazon customers in New York City were greeted with an Amazon Homepage announcing 'Amazon Magic'—a new standalone mobile app that gives customers free and fast scheduled same-day delivery (six 2-hour delivery slots between 9am and 9pm) on a huge selection of products. For $X.99, you can also select 'Presto!' an ultra-fast 1-hour delivery service... If you're one of the few people who have not signed up yet, you should try this out now."—Tech Crunch, Oct. 24th, 2014[2]

After the project moves further along the development process, the mock press release can be used as a compass to help keep the project on track. The product team can ask, "Are we building what is in the press release?" If not, they can re-evaluate their priorities.

The process of working backward is all about focusing on the customer's needs. Instead of starting with the product or technology they want to build, Amazon begins with a focus on what customers will love, and which problems their products can solve in their customers' lives. Working backwards can be difficult, but it's powerful when done right, and accounts for Amazon's profound success and customer loyalty.

This is an entrepreneurial approach from Amazon, and requires full investment and ownership from every party that's involved in each new project. This is an important element for brands to work into their own understanding of Amazon's ecosystem. Both Amazon and your company need to be agile and ahead of the market, as well as being robust and defensible, and working backwards is the best way for that to happen.

Working backwards from the specific outcomes and goals your company has set will save your team from getting distracted, buried in minutiae or from working on ideas that won't delight your customers. For some CMOs, working backwards is going to lead to some tough conversations: whether the company or team is structured effectively to reach the company's goals, whether existing processes are efficient enough, and whether the right people are in place. But, to work backwards ourselves, let's delve into what some of those outcomes and goals might look like.

The Hierarchy of Your Brand's Needs

When it comes to Amazon, most brands have multiple outcomes under consideration. There's the obvious goal of growing sales and increasing market share, but there are also several other major outcomes that should be factored in. These outcomes are all closely related, and each one affects the others, but there's a hierarchy of needs—you have to take care of the critical, foundational needs before you move on to loftier goals:

1. Brand Protection

One of the most common questions we are asked is about how companies can protect the brand they've developed over their years in operation. Most companies realize that they need a presence on Amazon, but they need to do it in such a way that they retain control of their positioning on the platform. Proactively managing resellers ensures that you retain control of the brand's presence on Amazon. This ensures you win the Buy Box, which in turn allows you to control the customer experience on the platform. Brand protection also includes controlling pricing, managing counterfeits, correcting inaccurate representations of your brand or products, and managing your brand and product content so that it's as accurate and engaging as possible.

2. Customer Experience

When you control the brand and consistently win the Buy Box, you also control how your brand looks, feels and sounds to customers across the entire Amazon ecosystem. You are able to shape the customer's experience and perception, and to provide them with the service and standards they have come to expect from you. In turn, this leads to greater customer satisfaction, more positive reviews and sales velocity, and therefore, greater exposure to new markets.

3. Operational Excellence

Getting your brand in front of Amazon's massive audience requires a very stable, reliable system for fulfilling customer orders and meeting customer expectations. Once you're hitting Amazon's strict standards for customer experience, your products and ads will be favored more by the search and display algorithms. Making your products Prime-eligible and ensuring your products are consistently in stock is part of this play.

4. Market Penetration

Once the foundational elements of your brand's presence on Amazon are taken care of, it's time to ramp up sales and capture more market share. Paid search advertising or PPC can be used effectively here to drive shoppers to your brand and product pages (and you can even target competitor brands or product terms to capture more market share). Product content that reinforces your brand's key messages for this new market should be built to drive conversions. Ultimately, if your products have a higher sales volume and conversion rate than competitors, you'll rank higher in organic search—and these two factors, when used effectively together, can help accomplish the goal of greater market penetration.

5. International Expansion

When your brand is really thriving on the US platform (or whichever is your home market), you can consider expanding your reach into international markets via Amazon's global infrastructure. When you've got full control of your brand, a productive relationship with resellers, a positive customer experience, and domestic market penetration, then you will be well-placed to replicate those successes globally.

But before we explore how to make all these outcomes a

reality, we need to take a moment to set some realistic expectations.

Setting Realistic Expectations About Amazon

There's a huge disconnect for many brands regarding the level of investment that's necessary to succeed with Amazon. The fact that Amazon used to be a scrappy start-up, or because some tools are still clunky, doesn't mean it's not an extremely sophisticated and complex system.

Many marketing executives need a major reset in their expectations around the investment, time and resources that will be necessary, particularly for those brands just embarking on their Amazon journey. In our experience, unfortunately, it's often only the companies who have been burned by mismanaging their initial investment that really understand the effort that's required. We want to use this section to highlight some specific expectations that may need adjustment before you chart a detailed course for your company's growth on Amazon.

The first thing to understand is that to make Amazon work as a sales and marketing channel, your company is going to have to commit to the investment that is required. As is the case with Facebook and Google, Amazon is a pay-to-play platform. It takes money, it takes people, and it often takes internal restructuring and budget redistribution. Many brands are reluctant to make the full commitment— they just want to add 'dealing with Amazon' into the job description for an existing role within the company.

The problem with this approach is that the designated person usually doesn't have any background in marketplace management, since it is a fairly nascent skillset. All too often we see junior employees left to figure it alone on top of their existing responsibilities and with no additional resourcing.

In reality, Amazon as a channel can function like an entire company in microcosm. For large brands, it's unrealistic to expect a single person to manage it all, because there's so much that goes into creating a successful Amazon strategy. There are so many elements to consider: item-level profitability, inventory and supply chain management, fulfilment, brand development, content marketing, advertising... these are all completely distinct skillsets that are usually handled by several different people (if not multiple teams). Even in mid-size companies, it's not appropriate or productive for all the responsibility for Amazon to fall exclusively on one person.

Beyond the personnel question, Amazon is still often underrepresented in budgeting. Amazon is a critical storefront, and it draws an enormous volume of traffic, so it's important to allocate significant budget to take full advantage of its capabilities, just as you would with your own DTC channel. This investment includes having proper creative and copy developed, resourcing an Amazon-specific customer support team, investing in media (particularly for new brands and products launching on the platform), and allocating a research and innovation budget that allows your product teams to take the data from Amazon and work backwards in developing customer-responsive products.

Attribution is another expectation that needs to be set accurately. Brands want to minimize wasted ad spend, see where their marketing spend is effective, and attribute sales as accurately as possible. But if you're going to invest in paid media across the walled gardens, you must acknowledge that you are never going to see a clear, end-to-end customer journey. It's fragmented, because none of the walled gardens (Amazon, Google, Facebook, etc.) have any interest in working with each other to provide that visibility. There is going to be waste and inefficiency between channels. That said, we're hopeful that this will improve over time: Amazon is building an end-to-end, closed loop marketing platform, providing top-of-funnel branding solutions, which will move customers all the way down the funnel to purchase, and then retarget customers to continue the cycle of commerce (and we'll discuss this more in Chapter 9).

Each of the walled gardens are designed to encourage brands to spend as much money within their walls as possible, but Amazon has the most compelling pitch for branded manufacturers here, since it owns the whole consumer purchase journey. It would be naïve and incorrect to say that all media spend should be allocated to Amazon and to ignore Facebook and Google to solve this problem—that's not going to happen, and nor should it. But it's also not advisable to spend large amounts of your resources trying to track every customer across all your platforms, trying to attribute every sale perfectly.

Most brands just want to accurately understand the return on their spend. If the spend is not delivering results, the data will show that there's a better solution. If it is working, the team knows where to focus their attention. While Amazon is not perfect, it offers better visibility on ROI and more control than we've seen on other platforms.

Finally, it's also important to set expectations about timing. If you expect significant sales within two weeks of setting up your Amazon storefront, you're going to be disappointed.

The first few months are about getting that flywheel spinning and picking up speed. For this to happen, everything in your account needs to be set up properly, and you need to budget time for testing, learning and gathering data about what is working. This timeline is going to be different to your team's previous experience—the time required to create some initial clickthrough on Google or sales through Facebook is just not enough to spin up the Amazon flywheel to where it's producing reliable sales.

Amazon might not deliver profitable sales while you're establishing your brand there in the short-term, so you have to think about it as a long-term play: it's probably more realistic to expect it to take six to twelve months to start performing at the level of your other channels.

Amazon is also not a one-size-fits-all platform. Jon Regala, Head of Sales and Business Development for Sony Mobile, pointed out that Amazon has a specific design for user experience, which means that you have just a few seconds to get your message across. That user flow is designed to ensure customers absorb as much information as possible while quickly scrolling through the feed, so it's key to craft your presence and message carefully—it doesn't work to just copy and paste all the material over from your DTC site and assume it will work the same way.

This all takes a lot of work, but the effort will be worth it. Amazon accounts for more than 50% of e-commerce sales in the United States. Prime alone has customers in *half* of all North American households, and Amazon's customers are brand-loyal to a degree we've really never seen before.

Ten or fifteen years ago, brands were resisting digital and underinvesting in their direct-to-consumer and e-commerce strategies. Today, in many cases, that resistance has shifted to Amazon, with brands undertaking slow transformations and underinvesting in their Amazon storefronts. In many cases, Amazon is not given an appropriate level of attention internally, but now is the time to correct this and position your company for continued success into the future.

Amazon As Part of A Multi-Channel Media Mix

Walled gardens—the major media platforms that control customer data—have exploded in the past decade and are incredibly powerful. At the time of writing, nearly 70% of all digital advertising dollars go to three walled gardens where the advertiser doesn't own the end customer.[3]

Along with Facebook and Google, Amazon has added significant complexity to the world of digital media and strategy, and these platforms are not at all incentivized to make things easier for marketers. The tools are sometimes clunky, we don't get much data back, they ultimately own the customer, and they don't communicate among themselves. There's little to no integration between platforms, which leaves the executives at brands of all sizes faced with a major problem: how do we attract and retain customers of our own without cannibalizing this channel or compromising the relationship with Amazon?

Brands don't want to miss out on the data and retargeting opportunities Amazon represents, but there's a tension in the relationship, and we'll explore how to navigate this issue throughout this chapter.

Leo Trautwein, interim CMO for a $100M dietary supplement company and former Vice President of E-Commerce and Strategic Development at Vista Outdoor, describes how he thinks about the potential cannibalization between channels:

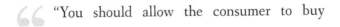 "You should allow the consumer to buy

wherever they want to buy. That's the true omni-channel perspective—if they want to buy on Amazon, they're going to buy on Amazon. If they want to buy in physical retail, or DTC, they will. So you have to differentiate the brand across these channels, so you're providing support to the customer wherever they are.

On our DTC site, of course, we should not be competing on price... Pricing should not be the criteria for the buying decision; consumers should make the decision on where they're going to buy based on the experience they're going to have, but DTC is our home, so everything should be perfect, or as close to it as we can get. From a content and information standpoint, everything has to be there: if a consumer wants to dig around and understand the brand, read the reviews, understand our policies, all those things have to be perfect in our home.

On our DTC channel, we look at whether there is anything we can offer that our partners cannot (because of their business model, not because we don't want them to offer it). That's where we started to do some interesting things with personalization, and on our DTC site we don't incentivize one-time purchase, we incentivize subscriptions, which is another way to differentiate from our retailers who are more focused on one-time sales. Those things are ways to generate interest without necessarily impacting the competition."

While Amazon has a long way to go before its advertising platform is at the same level of maturity and scale as Google and Facebook, it's growing rapidly and attracting both performance and brand marketing dollars. It's aggressively taking over market share in digital advertising, but as we've pointed out, most brands are still underspending.

For example, Mark had an experience with a brand where Amazon accounted for 30% of their total sales, but only 2% of their total media budget. From a total budget of $1.3 million, just $20,000 was allocated to spend on Amazon, despite the fact it was overperforming compared to their other channels. The client hadn't aligned their expectations appropriately, and were expecting Amazon to act as a magic bullet: they were hoping for an even higher sales velocity with their Amazon storefront, and hadn't realized that the growth was spectacular given how little investment they were making there.

Another client was selling a product *exclusively* on Amazon, but of their $100,000 marketing budget, less than $10,000 had been allocated to advertising on Amazon. The vast majority was going to Google and Bing—where the customer couldn't make a purchase and would be directed to Amazon anyway. Mark had them flip the budget, so they started spending 80% on Amazon ads instead, and their sales velocity started climbing immediately. While advertising on Google can still be worthwhile, if your product is exclusively sold on Amazon, it's far more effective to use Amazon's advertising data to target people who are already on the platform and are known to be in-market for that type of product.

There are many surveys of merchants who say that Amazon continues to offer the best value for PPC advertising across any search platform. Within the platform, cost per click *is* climbing, but compared to more established platforms, where there is much greater competition, it's often still more efficient to advertise on Amazon.

Part of this efficiency comes from the constraint that Amazon only sells physical items. On other paid search platforms you can advertise digital products, services, education, insurance and so on, but on Amazon's paid search advertising platform you can only advertise physical products. (Note that paid search advertising or PPC is different to Amazon's media platform or DSP, where non-endemic brands can advertise.)

Budget isn't the only consideration brands have to factor in when advertising with Amazon. In many cases, a bigger challenge occurs when your brand isn't well-known on Amazon—how do you build up brand awareness with Amazon's customers to actually make your spend effective? It doesn't make sense to allocate budget to search ads on Amazon, because if no one knows who you are, no one is searching for you.

And if you're in a competitive category, and no one is searching for your brand, why would you spend your budget on search? The vast majority of brands who do spend on Amazon are spending it on PPC (unofficial estimates from an Amazon insider suggested that only about 15% of sellers even use PPC). But there is so much more that brands can experiment with here. Instead of always building lower funnel advertising assets first, some brands do better with Amazon's advertising when they start by simply building customer awareness. Monica Ferguson, co-founder of Solemates, explained how her company has seen this strategy play out:

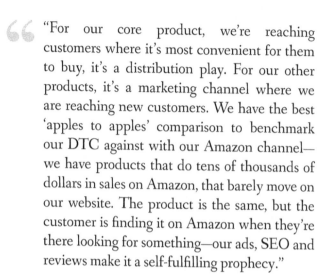

> "For our core product, we're reaching customers where it's most convenient for them to buy, it's a distribution play. For our other products, it's a marketing channel where we are reaching new customers. We have the best 'apples to apples' comparison to benchmark our DTC against with our Amazon channel—we have products that do tens of thousands of dollars in sales on Amazon, that barely move on our website. The product is the same, but the customer is finding it on Amazon when they're there looking for something—our ads, SEO and reviews make it a self-fulfilling prophecy."

As a brand building tool, Amazon has so much potential. Their advertising capabilities allow brands to target customers with display, video, custom executions, samples, trial boxes, Alexa and voice search, and that list is only getting longer.

For large brands that can't currently sell on Amazon, adopting search will be exciting if in the future Amazon allows search to deliver results beyond the products being sold on the platform, but there are already huge opportunities with the growth of Amazon's programmatic DSP. Brands in automotive, financial services and other non-endemic categories can use Amazon's data to target relevant audiences across Amazon's affiliated properties and its third-party advertising network, which has hundreds of properties.

This extensive buying data, combined with the knowledge of which customers are in-market for a certain product is a unique offering among the walled gardens, and is one way these brands can own the Amazon customer relationship. If you're not selling on Amazon (as a non-endemic brand), you can drive the traffic anywhere you want. And even if you do sell on Amazon as an endemic brand, they're slowly opening up the guidelines on this—you can now use its third-party network to drive traffic to your DTC site, though for now any ads you serve on the actual Amazon.com property still can't send users off-site.

Brand Building On Amazon

When we talk about brand building, we're referring to increasing the visual recognition customers have of your brand across Amazon properties, and the upper funnel tactics you can utilize to attract new audiences (as opposed to lower-funnel search and conversion tactics). Amazon has only had display and video inventory available for a few years, and the consoles to access that inventory have been clunky and challenging for marketers to use. But despite its lacklustre UI/UX interface and lack of integration, Amazon has a very sophisticated suite of marketing and advertising tools with unique benefits, and ambitious plans to integrate these into a single technology stack. Still, many marketers are still only thinking of Amazon as a product search mechanism.

A lot of companies are tripped up by an expectation that paid search on Amazon is going to be a cure-all for not having a strong brand. But if you're a real brand with the intent to differentiate yourself in the market, your advantage on Amazon is in your brand building capability.

Brand building is an area where teams can take some ownership, expand on what they are good at, and use Amazon's media capabilities as part of that strategy. National brands with larger budgets could potentially find a lot of success with a hybrid model here, by experimenting with different combinations of Amazon Advertising, subscription models and experiential events on the platform.

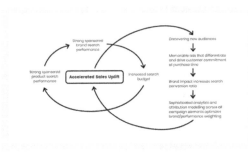

When you focus on the upper funnel—brand building, name recognition and so on—your lower funnel performance will also start to improve. When people start searching for your brand more often, your products will also start to show up more in search results and paid ad listings.

And whether or not you're selling on Amazon, there is ample opportunity to build brand awareness by leveraging its rich data set, and to drive those new audiences to your storefronts, product pages or other online experiences.

For example, there are automotive companies spending upwards of $30 million dollars on Amazon for brand awareness when they don't sell any of their core products on the platform. Ford, General Motors, and many other car companies all have dozens of products that are related to the cars customers are about to buy, they have incredible reviews, and they are aggressively taking advantage of Amazon's innovative brand building opportunities.

The customer lifecycle on Amazon is vastly different to every other platform and a challenge for brands to navigate. How do you take an initial engagement with a new Amazon customer, and transition them over the long-term to becoming an omni-channel brand advocate for you—not just a brand advocate on Amazon? Promotions like Prime Day, custom executions and experiential programs all allow brands to drive market awareness and to attract new buyers into the early stages of the purchase journey.

Andy Horrow, President of Protein20 and formerly the Head of Marketing at Tropicana and Gatorade, explained how his team has approached brand building on Amazon:

> "We think of Amazon as an awesome discovery vehicle for our product. So many consumers search for solutions on Amazon, without a specific idea of the product they are looking for. In that sense, our investment in Amazon is a marketing spend—a place to generate incredible targeted awareness for Protein20. Once a consumer is tracked as interested in our category or our brand, the Amazon model goes to work to initiate promotional reminders and subscribe-and-save opportunities to build repeat business. Protein20 has a 38% repeat buy rate now, which is outstanding."

Fulfilment Is A Marketing Decision

Integrating Amazon into your multi-channel sales strategy can be a complicated process—to make it fit in with your retailers, wholesalers, e-commerce store, and to integrate it smoothly into your logistics and operations. But there's an added element to this logistical question that many brands don't consider: how shipping and fulfilment impacts your success in the search and display rankings.

To begin with, let's call out the main mechanisms for fulfilling customer orders on Amazon.

If you're a Vendor selling to Amazon (on Vendor Central), you are generally filling wholesale Purchase Orders, shipping inventory directly to Amazon and having them process all the orders. Sometimes Vendors are required to drop-ship orders to customers, meeting certain fulfilment criteria that Amazon sets in your Vendor Terms. Under either scenario, all your products are Prime-eligible, which customers really care about, and dramatically increases conversions and overall sales velocity.

If you're selling on Seller Central, you have a few different options. The first option is to leverage Amazon's fulfilment infrastructure (Fulfilled by Amazon—'FBA'). You send inventory to Amazon, who store your inventory in their fulfilment centers, and then pick, pack and ship customer orders as they come through. Under this scenario, your products will be Prime-eligible.

The second option on Seller Central is to fulfil orders from your brand's facility and to send inventory directly to customers as they purchase, called Fulfilled By Merchant. Because Amazon views this as a less reliable option for the customer, those products don't get to be Prime-eligible, so you miss out on potential sales from customers who insist on buying Prime-eligible products. Many companies misunderstand how significant that delta is, and try to hold onto the profitability of using their own fulfilment infrastructure. But this can be a false economy when you consider that sacrificing some margin can result in a significant increase in sales volume. Kiri's agency has found that sales volume generally increases two to five times when a product becomes Prime-eligible.

The final option is the best and worst of both worlds—Seller-Fulfilled Prime, where sellers can fulfil orders directly through their own infrastructure to customers, *and* the products are Prime eligible. As appealing as this option is at first glance, being Prime-eligible means that all orders have to look, sound, and feel just like Prime, as delivered by Amazon itself. In today's environment, that means one-day shipping, which is extremely expensive for most brands to accommodate. Brands are expected to offer that free one-day shipping through FedEx (though maybe in the future, Amazon will have its own fulfilment capability), *and* you have to provide 99 to 100% on-time accuracy for deliveries.

This can be very difficult to comply with, simply because your brand doesn't control FedEx and you can't control for every contingency that might occur between dispatching the product and the customer receiving it. Amazon has extremely high expectations of what the customer should experience with Prime, which can make it difficult to meet the demands of the Seller-Fulfilled Prime program—brands that don't meet the requirements may have their SFP capabilities revoked and their items will not be Prime-eligible, so the stakes are high.

The point of outlining all these options is to highlight that—unless you're selling very bulky items for which customers expect a long delivery timeline, you're probably going to have to take a hit on your margins to get the most out of the platform and to offer a Prime experience for shoppers. Amazon rewards Prime eligibility through its algorithm and shoppers trust it more, and so your choice of fulfilment method here will reverberate throughout the rest of your strategy for the platform.

Of course, how you deliver orders is not the only logistical decision your brand is going to have to contend with. Some companies, especially in CPG, are set up to function exclusively as wholesale businesses. They're only set up to fulfil purchase orders, to ship pallets of product to stores or distributors who then break those bulk shipments up for individual sale. If Amazon is not interested in signing these brands up as a wholesale vendor, or if they decide that the marketplace offering suits them better, these companies have to figure out how to ship 'eaches'—individual items that individuals consumers order, one unit at a time.

For example, Kiri's agency works with a CPG company that sells packaged snacks, and it's an enormous logistical challenge for them to go from shipping pallets to being able to ship out a 24-pack to an individual consumer. This is also the case for high-volume apparel manufacturers, who have not historically needed processes in place to package, say, an individual dress.

In cases like this, deciding to sell on Amazon can require a reconfiguration of the entire infrastructure of the business. John Halverson, Vice President of Global Media, Digital & Data for Mondelez International, shared one example of how their business has had to reconfigure to adapt to Amazon's demands:

 "When we started getting into this space, our famous Advent calendars for Christmas were designed to be just one inch too big for Amazon's packaging in the UK. They weren't going to get carried, because they couldn't be shipped. So we had to rethink the product from the ground up—you can't design something that's too big for a standard Amazon box or packaging, because they won't carry it. Amazon has changed how we think about price-pack architecture, how we think about which packaging to put forward, and how we design products and packaging specifically for e-commerce. This has been super important."

Again, this is why the executive branch of each company needs to lead these decisions: establishing your organization on this platform can have far-reaching effects throughout the entire business, and it will require cohesive leadership, vision and resourcing to see your strategy through to success.

SIX

ORGANIZATIONAL DESIGN IN AN AMAZON WORLD

Amazon Leadership Principle: Dive Deep

"Leaders operate at all levels, stay connected to the details, audit frequently, and are skeptical when metrics and anecdotes differ.
No task is beneath them."

THE MOST EFFECTIVE way to guide the development of your organization's Amazon strategy is to stick as closely as possible to this leadership principle. As we've said, Amazon is a microcosm of the entire business, and because a successful Amazon strategy will touch so many parts of an organization (finance, product, brand, marketing, sales, fulfilment, customer service, etc.), the CMO and the team overseeing Amazon need to immerse themselves in the platform and commit to creating organization-wide progress.

They need to be able to ask questions, make big decisions, and to advocate for the Amazon channel and customer.

Too often, responsibility for Amazon is pushed onto someone who is working in a silo in some dark corner by themselves or juggling it as one of their many priorities, and who is not a key decision-maker with a voice in the organization. The people leading this transformation should have the authority and visibility to make this channel thrive. Without this force, Amazon often continues to be deprioritized, which means it lacks the necessary investment, and the business misses a critical strategic opportunity.

Any CMO worth their salt cannot afford to have Amazon sitting on the periphery of their strategy. The reason this chapter opens with the Dive Deep principle is that Amazon does not belong to a single department within any organization. The CMO will need to take a deep dive into the platform and the strategic options that are open to them, in order to understand how their organization needs to develop their approach to Amazon, and what to expect success to look like in the future. CMOs need a clear sense of who they will need to draw into this process, and what will be required to lead their company to success.

This deep dive will enable you to identify what makes Amazon tick, what it takes to be successful as a seller, marketer and media buyer in that ecosystem, and how to look at Amazon as a platform that's continuing to expand and connect with hundreds of millions of consumers across many different touchpoints. If leaders don't embrace that— if they refuse to see it as anything other than just another line item on a media plan, or as just another distribution channel—they are actively ignoring a lucrative opportunity, which may negatively impact the long-term growth of their company.

Now, many large companies have complained that their brands have only just finished going through a 'digital transformation'—getting everything set up to grow and market their brands effectively online. And while it might feel like you've barely had time to catch your breath, that first transformation will likely have created many of the systems, teams, reporting lines, mandates and infrastructure you will need for your company's 'Amazon transformation'. As you know, Amazon has become much broader and much more significant than it was a few years ago, both as a media platform and a sales channel. Technology is moving so fast that you can't afford to fall behind at this moment—if you can rally your organization to tackle this transformation now, rather than putting it off a couple more years, you'll be in a good position to take advantage of all the opportunities Amazon presents, and to attract the talent that will help you capitalize on it.

It's also important to understand that an Amazon transformation is not going to be a 'one and done' activity. While many of the necessary pieces will now be in place, some parts of your organization may need to be retooled for this. Your winning strategy will take time to be realized and to deliver profitable sales, and for the workflow around the Amazon ecosystem to settle into predictable patterns. As we said earlier, Amazon's ecosystem changes constantly. There are frequent updates, new initiatives and programs launched regularly, and a steady stream of new challenges and opportunities sprinkled in for good measure.

There's a transformation on two fronts: there's the internal, structural transformation that has to happen amongst the leadership and teams that are formulating and executing the Amazon strategy for the brand; and then there's the customer-facing marketplace transformation, where companies are committing to new sales channels, products and branding.

For brands that identify that Amazon is indeed a strategic imperative and choose to respond proactively, there will be an increase in budget, resources and attention. All these elements bring increased scrutiny and account-ability, so it's key to set yourself up from the beginning to deliver on those expectations with the right partners, talent and structure.

This structural transformation takes time, because if you have a team that is already handling Amazon, they will also need to be resourced differently. It can't go from being a side project to being a strategic imperative without the structure and resources around the existing team changing too.

This structural transformation also impacts your DTC presence: for many brands, their existing DTC site is an important source of sales, with SEO equity that has been built up over several years (along with processes and talent for keeping the site and brand up to date). Brands have existing brand channels that need to avoid conflict with Amazon, and few companies want to slow down DTC sales while they build up their marketplace presence. CMOs and their teams have to navigate listing products on Amazon, building new product pages, content, and customer experi-ences—whilst avoiding a dip in sales across their other channels.

It's just as challenging for traditional companies that don't sell DTC. Companies that primarily sell to national accounts are often unaccustomed to providing individual customer support, creating consumer-facing content, and building engaged audiences for their brand and products. They're used to marketing to retailers, and providing content and information for retailers to use at POS. Writing copy for online product pages is a completely different skillset to writing descriptions for wholesale catalogs, and as we mentioned earlier, just thinking about how to handle selling individual units to customers is a huge transformation for some companies.

For this transformation to happen, both structurally within the organization and in their approach to the marketplace, there's got to be a clear sense of ownership among the team. While it's difficult to develop a sense of ownership by top-down mandate, the leadership does need to be clear in communicating to every employee and partner what's important, what the imperatives are, and how they expect everybody to execute the strategy.

Now is not the time to lay blame for things that haven't worked previously, to avoid responsibility, or to cling to the justification that because everything keeps changing, it's too hard to try anything new. Yes, things change fast, and that reality is here to stay. Everyone in your organization needs to understand that there's no one at Amazon to hold your hand, that the strategy and tactics will have to evolve constantly, and that to thrive in this environment, the whole team will have to embrace this opportunity wholeheartedly.

Who Is Accountable For Amazon?

In a profile for *Digiday*, Giovanni Colavita, CEO of Colavita USA (a CPG brand which sells Italian-sourced products like olive oil, tomato sauce, pastas and chocolates) shared his insightful approach to building his Amazon team and strategy. He said that when the company first decided to sell on Amazon in 2010, he decided to build a "non-traditional" retail team immediately, with capabilities in e-commerce, social media and marketing. Instead of waiting for the channel to show major growth, Colavita USA hired an SEO manager, a graphic designer, and a social media and digital marketing team. Colavita also said it was critical that they prepared both manufacturing and e-commerce teams for unanticipated growth, since orders could vary from 10 cases to 1,000 cases from week to week based on consumer demand.

When growth on Amazon and other marketplaces started to outpace sales on their DTC site in 2014, Colavita decided to stop investing in the DTC site and to focus deeply on Amazon and other marketplaces. Since then, Colavita has become the top-selling olive oil on Amazon, with about 50% of the Colavita Group's total $250 million in annual sales coming from e-commerce. At the time of writing, Colavita was projecting an increase in e-commerce sales for the year ahead in the triple digits, with significant increases in brick-and-mortar sales—and Colavita credits their innovative team structure with this explosive growth. He said that creating a nimble team that could handle the dynamic Amazon environment was key to creating a defensible brand that is protected from any sudden changes Amazon might decide to implement.

"Regardless of whether you're running your own e-commerce or not, you need to have a team in place that can handle e-commerce," said Colavita. "That's not a traditional team. You will never succeed online with traditional sales and customer service—it's like trying to do business in two different countries, with one team."[1]

AMAZON CAN FIT within several divisions at most

companies, though it's been most common to see responsibility allocated exclusively to sales, marketing or e-commerce. Sales seems to have been the most common option, because Amazon was treated as a sales account, with the salespeople selling into Amazon the same way they would sell into Krogers or Nordstroms, with the same resources and attention as all their other sales channels. But because companies don't usually allocate a big marketing budget to the sales department, these teams couldn't invest in the product content, advertising, and customer service necessary to really make the channel thrive.

If that's the case in your company, you'll likely get better results by reworking the organizational design here, either creating a whole new Amazon (or marketplace) team, or bringing Amazon under the marketing team's remit where you can best control the brand's positioning on the platform and where there is usually more budget available to invest.

This shift in the organizational design also reflects how influential Amazon can be in brand media and performance marketing strategies. In large companies, brand media and performance marketing are often treated separately. (Performance marketing campaigns and tactics drive lower funnel activity, where you're engaging with customers at the platform level to generate clicks and conversions. Brand media is about upper funnel activity—generating brand awareness and market education to attract customers into the purchase journey). But media teams are often still coordinating with large external agencies and overseeing large budgets that haven't factored in an appropriate spend for Amazon, and now many of those teams are scrambling to find incremental spend they can reallocate.

Amazon can also fit into the remit of the e-commerce

team, and in some companies has been siloed there, with relatively junior 'digital natives' hacking away to make the channel perform without any real structure or strategy. At this moment, though, when Amazon is accounting for over 50% of total e-commerce sales and growing, this structure is no longer viable and a new approach is required.

Companies of all sizes are realizing that they need a specific leader within the organization to take clear responsibility for Amazon. You need one senior executive responsible for rallying everyone in the organization around a shared, holistic strategy that coordinates media, marketing, sales, product, finance and every other division that Amazon touches. There has to be one person that runs point and is the central facilitator for this part of the business; otherwise, no one has ownership and important things will be missed.

This executive sponsorship is critical, because when it comes down to the practical decisions on investment, resources, and making sacrifices now to benefit the company later, someone in the room must be able to make a final call and drive the transformation through. Another Amazon leadership principle is Bias For Action—working quickly to grasp an advantage—so this person should not be at board level, as requiring board approval for decisions takes too long. This needs to be a senior executive who can make operational decisions on a day-to-day basis.

Here's how John Halverson, Vice President of Global Media, Digital & Data at Mondelez, described this to us:

> "If I were designing an organization, I would put Amazon with a Chief Growth Officer, because the CGO has responsibility across marketing, sales, and digital. You have to have

control of price-pack architecture, which is why it's often an executive relationship. When people try to manage Amazon as simply a media relationship, or just a sales relationship, they're not capturing the value and they're not maximizing the opportunity. Whoever owns the relationship with Amazon, the key thing is about the talent, and the ability to move with speed, make decisions and influence every part of the system."

This executive has to be able to wrangle all the key stakeholders within the company and ensure that the right people are involved to the appropriate degree. If you are that executive, you have to 'speak the language' of each of those people. Fortunately, Amazon provides metrics and reports that will address the interests and concerns of most stakeholders, and you can rely on this extensively to make the business case to each party to ensure the right organizational design and resourcing for your Amazon strategy.

For example, if you approach the CFO and say, "We've been underinvesting in Amazon—we've been growing at 20% year over year with no investment, and I think it could be 40%. Here's the margin we're getting, here is how accretive this channel is, here's the evidence that these are new customers that are not being cannibalized from other channels"—then that's going to be a good case to help you get increased budget for the channel. If you can take a relevant business case, supported by data, to your customer service division, and say, "Here's how many Amazon enquiries we get per week, our average response time is X and that's too slow according to Amazon's requirements; here are the sales consequences of that delay"—then you're going to be able to make a strong argument for an increased budget and resources.

Once you get a handle on the metrics that are important to each stakeholder, you will be able to present a customized business case to each of them. This will help stakeholders feel that their priorities are being recognized and should make them more willing to work with you towards outcomes that benefit the entire company.

Amazon As An Investment

Compared to other walled gardens like Google and Facebook, Amazon's metrics can be slow to respond to drastic increases in ad spend, because it takes time for sales to be attributed to advertising. Unfortunately, brands can't just throw more media dollars at Amazon and double their money overnight, or expect to see really aggressive growth within weeks or even months. It takes time and patience to see your investment come to fruition, and so this needs to be factored in when your organization is deciding where the money for this investment will come from in the first place. Does the budget for this transformation come from the overall media investment of the brand? Should it come from marketing, from sales, or should every division contribute some of their budget? What percentage of spend should be allocated there?

There's no hard rule for any of this, but we believe that the budgeting decisions have to be made at the C-suite level, where a corporate budget can be carved out for investing in the platform. Leo Trautwein, interim CMO for a $100M dietary supplement company and former Vice President of E-Commerce and Strategic Development at Vista Outdoor, told us that at many companies he works with, Amazon falls into his 'new initiatives' budget:

> "I always save part of my budget for those advertising initiatives that can generate new interest, which I will call experiments. Typically it's around 10% of the budget, but it can even be up to 15%. I will put that money towards new things, and new things might not be new to the market, but new to us, things we have never done before. Then it's a matter of just testing them. I keep this 10 or 15% to try new things, we try at a smaller scale, and if it brings a good return, then we start scaling that up for the remainder of the year. Then if it really proves valuable for the rest of the year, it becomes part of my regular budget. There are things in that process that just fail, not everything works, but that's how I treat testing."

This is a different approach to how most brands decide on their annual budgets, which might be based on the previous year's KPIs, plus or minus a few percentage points based on performance. And while we believe that 10% of every brand's budget should be invested into testing new initiatives to capture and scale growth opportunities in the future, what about those companies whose marketing and media budget is, say, $800 million? Good luck securing approval to spend $80 million on experiments. While some agile and progressive companies can be experimental to that degree, for most, it's difficult to justify spending that much on test-and-learn projects. Regardless, companies do need to carve out money for innovation, even if it's only a small percentage of their total budget to begin with.

In most progressive companies, Amazon is no longer seen as an innovation play, but the questions remain: How do you innovate in a marketplace where consumers are considering your products and comparing them with our competitors? How do you make those products more appealing? How do you differentiate your brand from an experiential perspective? How do you use Amazon as a branding platform?

This is why these decisions (about what the budget will be and who has responsibility for Amazon) must come down from the C-suite, where there is sufficient authority to allocate resources and drive the strategy forward.

The New Marketplace Responsibilities

When we're talking about organizational design, some companies are designating a role to be responsible exclusively for marketplaces, and even, in some cases, just for Amazon. While small companies may want to add marketplaces into someone's existing responsibilities, for other brands it makes sense to have a role that is entirely focused on this area, or at least to create C-suite accountability for it.

There is a new position that's emerging in medium and large sized companies called the Marketplace Director or the Head of Marketplace. We expect marketplaces to become a whole new sales function, because while Amazon is dominating that space right now, we're already seeing other marketplace platforms emerging and growing, and these will become increasingly important in the sales and marketing strategies of companies of all sizes.

One such example is Byron Kerr, now Head of Amazon

at mattress company Tuft & Needle. Kerr explained that for many companies, no one has direct responsibility for Amazon, and that because various people work on it in across marketing, product and supply chain, brands end up with a messy, tag-team approach that suffers from a lack of resources. He went on to say that eventually, someone has to take ownership of Amazon, because as the brand starts to scale there, it becomes necessary to secure dedicated resources, and to have a leader with experience growing brands to lead a growing team of specialists.

It's worth exploring this option early in your company's transformation, because as Jeff Bezos has pointed out, Amazon is not beyond being disrupted by other marketplaces.

As huge a company as Amazon is now, they've continued to be innovative, and have thus far avoided the Innovator's Dilemma (where a brand starts out as a disruptor, then becomes so successful that they become the incumbent and stop innovating). To date, Amazon's Day One focus has prevented complacency and bureaucracy from setting in, so it seems more likely that disruption will come from outside in the form of regulation and increased competition, rather than through internal complacency.

Amazon has become so powerful in retail that they are facing a lot of political pressure to keep their divisions separate. They've come under a lot of scrutiny for how much influence they wield over the entire retail supply chain, since they're no longer just a distribution channel. Now that Amazon is also a marketing channel, a product manufacturer, and a brokerage channel, antitrust concerns are becoming more and more prevalent. This, in turn, opens the door to more marketplace competition, and other companies are already pursuing this aggressively.

Competition is coming in from multiple sources, both from aggregated marketplaces and from individual DTC companies that have achieved success in delighting customers and creating a frictionless purchase journey. There are new payment models and commerce tools being developed all the time; social media and search giants are trying to disrupt DTC e-commerce. Retail giants, both online and offline, are brawling for market share, and while marketplaces competing with Amazon are currently behind, the catch-up isn't going to take long and will only benefit consumers even more.

This is why the Head of Marketplace role is becoming so important: having someone internal in your company ensures that you always have eyes on what's happening in the marketplace world, and that you are positioned to take advantage of new opportunities as they arise: everyone wants a piece of the action, and we're under no illusions that Amazon is the only place you should be selling. It's growing quickly and is not showing any signs of slowing down, but we do expect that there will be a levelling-off in the growth of Amazon's core marketplace over the next few years as competition catches up.

And while you might not think of Walmart and Target as innovative companies, they absolutely are, and are both investing heavily to get an edge in this space. Both companies now offer Prime-esque memberships with one-day shipping and special offers. With the exception of Amazon's grocery footprint with Whole Foods, these other retailers also have the added advantage of people physically walking into stores, where they're building out medical services, and offering products (such as insurance and finance) that don't fit an online sales model.

There's been speculation that, ironically, Walmart is

best placed to slow Amazon's meteoric rise, because they offer a large range of products with a layer of scrutiny over merchants that Amazon doesn't have. There's less counterfeiting and less grey areas for sellers with Walmart, and it's the same with Target's marketplace platform.

So if you know that your customer is a Target customer, for example, and you've had a good relationship with them in the past, continue to focus on that segment. It's going to be to your advantage, particularly when it's done in parallel with your Amazon growth strategy and your plans for establishing your brand on other emerging marketplaces.

Like the digital transformation, the Amazon transformation is a dynamic process and will likely shift into an overall marketplace transformation. This transformation requires ongoing investment, adaptation and innovation, and as is the case in most business scenarios, you're going to need the best talent you can find to maximize your success.

SEVEN

PICK YOUR PEOPLE: TALENT & PARTNERS

Amazon Leadership Principle:
Hire and Develop the Best

"Leaders raise the performance bar with every hire and promotion. They recognize exceptional talent, and willingly move them throughout the organization. Leaders develop leaders and take seriously their role in coaching others. We work on behalf of our people to invent mechanisms for development like Career Choice."

TO UNDERSTAND how to approach building your own talent pool to work on Amazon, it helps to understand Amazon's work culture and how their focus on talent has affected how the company developed. Right from the start, Jeff Bezos implemented the 'two-pizza rule' to keep teams small and scrappy, believing that if you can't feed your team with two pizzas on a late-night work session, then you've got too many people on the team. This attitude is driven by the belief that in order to move quickly, you need to have nimble teams working on multiple projects simultaneously.

Given that Amazon has grown astronomically over the past 25 years, their relentless commitment to hiring the best and brightest has obviously worked for them. But the downside of having so many small teams empowered to create new ventures and make decisions is that there are hundreds, maybe thousands of teams working on different initiatives, in pursuit of different objectives.

This is one of the biggest complaints we hear from companies trying to navigate their own Amazon growth: sometimes it feels like there's very little continuity or transparency across Amazon's organization. This can make it hard to coordinate your own efforts: for example, if you have a vendor manager, they won't be able to tell you what's going with your media spend, and if you can get in touch with the paid search team, they won't be able to tell you anything about expected future purchase orders.

Amazon has traditionally required a specialist skillset for users to really leverage its offerings, and early on, the skills necessary to make the most of its features weren't clearly defined. People were thrown into this new environment and had no option but to be resourceful and adaptable. There were no official best practices and individual early adopters had to find their own way, relying on peers and the broader Amazon seller community for guidance, with many adopting their own test-and-learn approach.

Even agencies who specialized early in dealing with Amazon had to iterate towards success, with limited resources and guidance. While these days there is a lot of tactical content available online, it's only very recent that

Amazon itself has started investing in producing best-practice content and official certifications to empower people to use their platform effectively.

Even for people with deep expertise on other channels, Amazon is much more complex to learn than most of the other walled gardens or platforms. Not only do users have to become familiar with the advertising tools, but they need to master inventory management, search, fulfilment, all the various policies and rules (and there are many). This requires a very motivated and resourceful type of talent.

Charlie Cole, Chief Global E-Commerce at Samsonite and Chief Digital Officer at Tumi explained that a good team needs to balance analytical pragmatism with the awareness that your brand is a living organism that will evolve over time, and that requires care in its handling. The people who will be most effective in these roles are not the type to just stay in their lane and do one thing well. These hires should be confident wearing multiple hats, and must comfortable with learning constantly, and being adaptable. Ultimately, your talent needs to be able to 'hack' Amazon to make a strategy work for as long as they can, and then iterate (or start fresh) when that strategy starts faltering.

These people should also know how to get a lot done with few resources—this is how Amazon operates, and it will help your people to have a consistent outlook and expectation about how the work on Amazon gets done. This is expressed in another one of Amazon's leadership principles— frugality: *"Accomplish more with less. Constraints breed resourcefulness, self-sufficiency, and invention. There are no extra points for growing headcount, budget size, or fixed expense."*

In their Retail division, Amazon aspires to a 'hands off the wheel' approach with their smaller brands and suppliers, expecting them to be fully responsible for their own processes on the platform—without the intervention or assistance of a Vendor Manager. While large brands that are important to Amazon's success may be rewarded with responsive Vendor Managers, Amazon generally wants their retail operation to be as automated as possible, and they prioritize removing human resources from processes if they're not absolutely essential.

This goes from managing the relationships with brands all the way down to having robots staffing the warehouses: Amazon is committed to running as lean as possible, so you're not going to get a whole lot of support. The burden has really shifted to brands to run their own accounts. And whereas Google and Facebook have fully empowered their clients to self-serve (their consoles and platforms are very mature, easy to use and have advanced support models), Amazon's self-service tools are more difficult to navigate and have many moving components that need to be operated in concert to achieve success.

Understanding that this burden is on your team can be challenging, especially for big manufacturers who are used to having deep working relationships with their key partners and distributors. Larger brands who generate tens or hundreds of millions of dollars in revenue on Amazon may have account managers, but for the vast majority of brands who generate less revenue, their only avenue for communicating with Amazon is often to contact the Seller Central support team.

This means that your team has to take full responsibility for your assortment planning, product development, marketing, advertising, and every other function on the platform, (or work with agency partners who can assist). You're not going to have a buyer telling you which products are going to do well, or what they want to buy from you. It's all driven by data, and increasingly, Amazon is expecting the brands to make those decisions around product development and inventory positions independently. This is why choosing the right internal hires, agency partners and consultants is so important—they will help your brand navigate this demanding environment effectively.

Your Amazon A-Team

One of the most common misconceptions we see with brands who are expanding their Amazon capability is the belief that hiring ex-Amazonians is going to give them an edge. That's not to say that the people who come out of Amazon aren't excellent—they are, because Amazon hires great people. Amazon has a very fast-paced work environment; they're very selective about who they hire and who advances, so those people are going to be very smart, persistent and hard-working. But because Amazon operates in silos, most employees only develop a deep knowledge of one specific part of the ecosystem. Ex-Amazonians are highly specialized in a way that may not be the right fit for every company, which means that there is a potential false economy in hiring people who used to work at Amazon.

Mark's agency, Podean, has two ex-Amazonians on the advertising team, and they've been exceptional additions to the business. But like any other hire, the experience is key: hiring someone just because they previously worked at Amazon won't mean they will be a silver bullet who can "just run the channel" for you. You wouldn't hire an ex-vendor manager to run your PPC, or an ex-advertising executive to create inventory projections or to handle disputed chargebacks, and the same principle applies to people who have come out of a specific role at Amazon. Of course, at the executional layer, a level of familiarity with the platform is important, but it will be difficult to find people who know everything about every element. Even within a specific part of Amazon (say, advertising), there are so many different areas of expertise that no one person can be totally across all of them.

Someone who is an expert in Google Adwords *could* transition fairly easily to working on Amazon's Sponsored Ads products, for example, because they are familiar with cost-per-click search advertising. However, consider the opportunity cost of growing that talent internally—a lot of brands think this skill adaptation will happen a lot faster than is realistic.

There hasn't been a whole lot of training or resourcing available for brands to actually upskill their internal teams and to ensure they are working according to current best practices. To overcome this, Kiri built the Marketplace Institute as a platform for brands to develop their own internal capabilities while still leveraging the best practices of an agency that has been delivering Amazon solutions for several years, and there's more information about this towards the end of this book for CMOs who want to develop their existing talent.

Whether you hire someone experienced, train someone up internally, or find specialist partners, don't get stuck thinking you need absolute expertise in every area to set your strategy in motion. You just need to give full responsibility and empowerment to the people you do choose, and to make sure they are aligned to the long-term plan.

For many large brands, it makes sense to work with external partners to develop and implement their Amazon strategy. The right partners will be able to help you define your long- and short-term objectives, identify the skillsets you have internally and those you need to supplement, and which of Amazon's programs are going to be most appropriate to help you reach your goals.

Foremost among these conversations should be how paid media fits into your overall Amazon growth strategy, and to develop clarity around the investment, time and iteration that's required for effective media planning and execution.

Choosing the right media agency is maybe the most important step in this process. Media agencies exist to handle media strategy and activation at scale—when your budget is in the multi-million dollar range, that's where an agency should come in to create effective strategy whilst achieving maximum efficiency for every dollar spent. They will be accountable for that budget, and for scaling the media appropriately in alignment with the brand's evolution.

However, it's important to be clear on whether you want accountability for that budget to be internal or external. Maintaining accountability internally is very different to handling it with external agencies. If someone doesn't deliver internally, you just have to regroup and adjust course. But if an agency doesn't deliver, there's further recourse, because you are paying for their service.

You also need to select agencies that can prove they can be collaborative—not just with your internal team, but with your other partners too. It is critical that the agency responsible for your media is willing to get on a call with your other agencies and openly discuss what's going on. If you have agencies in silos, it quickly becomes very inefficient and disorganized, because everyone ends up working against each other. Every party needs to have dialogue and to be able to work together. Your Amazon 'point person' needs to be the central conduit for that, but all the external partners have to be willing to collaborate right from the start of the relationship.

Many major agencies have been slow to react to Amazon, having spent years developing their Google and Facebook partnerships and offerings, whilst building out other digital capabilities. In many cases, Amazon has taken them by surprise, and smaller Amazon specialist agencies have been able to capitalize on this lag. Whatever agency you choose to partner with, the CMO has to anticipate potential inefficiencies and to hold partners accountable to deliver the performance they promise. It's important to be clear on what you want to achieve, and on what timeline.

There are any number of ways you can configure this, and you don't have to stick with a single model. You can change how you resource your Amazon strategy as the strategy itself evolves over time—maybe agencies can fill the gap while you upskill internally, or maybe they can take over once your team reaches their upper limit. Either way, collaborative partners and talent are absolutely critical if your strategy is going to be successful.

Creating An Integrated Strategy Whilst Navigating Amazon's Siloes

Creating an integrated strategy for your organization when Amazon itself is so siloed is admittedly a challenge. This is why we're so focused on who has overall responsibility for Amazon within the organization. This person will be responsible for evaluating and selecting partners who can help execute the plans, provide proactive strategic guidance to the team, and keep an eye on where the future is going with Amazon. It is also critical to identify partners that will help you optimize your presence and dominate your category as much as possible (and the senior leader accountable for Amazon will also be responsible for making these external parties accountable).

It's wise to build your e-commerce team to be dynamic and adaptable, just as Colavita did, because in addition to Amazon, you're going to need a general marketplace strategy within the next couple of years. The brands that have an experienced, cohesive team in place as those opportunities arise will thrive as marketplaces become more prevalent.

So when it comes to hiring, focus on strategy first. The people you need early on are those who can create practical, realistic goals, and can imagine what the future is going to be like. That strategic leadership (and the mindset that goes with it) delivers a combination of experience, the ability to formulate a clear, actionable plan, and the ability to coordinate that plan's execution. Sarah LaVallee, formerly E-Commerce Director of I and Love and You, and now Vice President of E-Commerce of Wandering Bear Coffee, shared her view on why this capability is so important:

> "Rallying the organization and getting everyone to understand why Amazon is important is key, because it's only then that operations, for example, will understand why they should be adapting their process to label individual units for sale to Amazon, or why should they look at creating a variety pack. They need to understand that the e-commerce shopper is different from the brick-and-mortar shopper. As the person that has ownership of

Amazon for your brand, you need to be grabbing all the different business units by the shoulders and getting them to take it seriously, to show them that if you do it right, it's going to pay off."

Once there's a clear plan, you can start hiring and delegating parts of the plan to various talent across your organization. First there's the logistical side—finding people to handle operations (including responding to customer messages, product reviews, seller feedback and so on), inventory planning, fee auditing (making sure you're getting the correct charges and revenue from Amazon), and brand protection (determining who is allowed to sell your products, who is not, and policing that).

Then there's the marketing side, where key responsibilities will be content, optimization and brand development. Performance marketing on Amazon is a very specific skillset, and for that reason it's probably the role that's most frequently outsourced—it benefits immensely from having an external partner who is solely focused on it. And finally, there's display and video advertising, along with the various other advertising solutions that Amazon offers.

We advise against having one person doing all of these varied and important tasks. Each role requires completely different skills, experience and pay grades (for example, it is not a good use of your e-commerce strategist's time to be responding to product reviews).

Depending on the size of the channel and how much volume there is, it might be necessary to hire several people in each of those areas. If you have a customer service team, your Amazon customer service may need to be built into a separate team that eventually handles all your marketplace support. In every organization, all this works a little bit differently. There's often a blend of internal people handling certain tasks and external partners handling others, and most organizations have to test and learn to find the approach that works best for their situation.

Choosing Your Strategists

Byron Kerr, Head of Amazon at Tuft & Needle, shared his approach to choosing external partners and vendors to work with his internal Amazon team:

> "When I look at the landscape of consultants, software and agencies, I don't think there's one right approach to managing your business. I think a hybrid approach is what's been most successful for me, where you can own some of the internal management, especially around marketing and leveraging software tools for automation... leveraging experts will allow you to gain insights that you may not find in your day-to-day experience. If you're having a challenge [with strategic decisions], that's where consultants and agencies really provide value, to pull back the curtain a bit, so that when you're going to market on the Amazon platform, you have all the necessary knowledge to make the best decision for your business."

Your strategic partners don't necessarily have to be Amazon experts. When Facebook took off, for example, companies trying to leverage its growth didn't hire social media experts, as very few existed. They hired clever people who could think laterally, were able to analyze data, and extrapolate the relevant ideas. It doesn't have to be your normal business strategist or consultant either. The right partner will understand the complexity of this space, have experience planning good outcomes for brands and will be able to work backwards to find the best solution, testing and learning along the way. The ability to collaborate is critical, in order to bring together all the different functions that are involved in delivering a successful Amazon strategy.

In addition to being collaborative, strategic partners should be open-minded, flexible and agile. They should have a test-and-learn mindset, a high tolerance for risk, and entrepreneurial spirit that gives them confidence to try new things on the platform. It's also important that they are willing to quickly adapt when something isn't working, and have a 'hacker mentality' that allows them to take in ideas from different sources and work with limited resources to find the right way forward.

If your strategic partner is internal, they should be senior enough to make independent decisions and to lead other people in a practical way. They don't need ultimate seniority in the organization but it's important that they can be responsible and empowered. External partners can also be great for this role, and agencies are often very well-placed to offer strategic guidance. They have a depth of expertise and strategic talent, who have worked across dozens of different brands in dozens of different categories. External partners are also able to see when Amazon changes much faster than you can on your own, simply because they have eyes on so many accounts.

But even if you do work with external partners who can give you that strategic insight, you still need an internal point person. This role is to coordinate communication between all your partners and stakeholders, and they'll need to be able to synthesize the intelligence coming in from agencies, and coordinate that with the needs and goals of the organization.

EIGHT

FUTURE OPPORTUNITIES & CONSIDERATIONS

Amazon Leadership Principle: Learn and Be Curious

"Leaders are never done learning and always seek to improve themselves. They are curious about new possibilities and act to explore them."

MORE THAN ANYTHING, Amazon is about innovation. Both as a company, and as a marketplace, they value testing and learning extremely highly. As a result, they are constantly evolving, pursuing new ideas and creating new opportunities. For any brand that's looking to continue growing and innovating into the future, it's important to understand the primary strategic framework that drives this culture of innovation forward.

Jeff Bezos has always been a powerful proponent of the Day One business outlook, and it's been absorbed into the company's daily drivers. This is a powerful framework for staying relevant and vigilant. Every successful startup begins with a solution to some problem, focusing on what the consumer needs, and what they want—even if they don't know it yet.

Bezos suggests that strong trends are not hard to spot in today's world. Many big companies get caught up in what has worked for them in the past instead of embracing what they could achieve today and into the future. That's what Day One is all about—maximizing every day by searching for ways to stay relevant to your customers. In a 2016 letter to shareholders, Bezos outlined the following four keys for maintaining a Day One mentality:

- True Customer Obsession: Even when they don't yet know it, customers want something better, and your desire to delight customers will drive you to invent on their behalf."
- Resist Proxies: "As companies get larger and more complex, there's a tendency to manage by proxies. This comes in many shapes and sizes, and it's dangerous, subtle, and very Day Two."
- Embrace External Trends: "Big trends are not that hard to spot (they get talked and written about a lot), but they can be strangely hard for large organizations to embrace."
- High-Velocity Decision Making: "Day Two companies make high-quality decisions, but they make high-quality decisions slowly. To keep the energy and dynamism of Day One, you have to somehow make high-quality, high-velocity decisions."[1]

Amazon is always innovating. Its people come in every day and say, *"OK, fresh start—what are the opportunities we haven't seen yet? What is the information hidden in the data? What can we do that's fresh and new?"* They are continually building, continually pushing forward, and brands will thrive when they cultivate this way of thinking within their own organizations.

Ultimately, cultivating a Day One attitude is about treating every day that you go to work with the energy and open mind that you brought to your first day on the job. In that frame of mind, you're not being complacent, you're doing the best work you can with the information and resources you have, you're focused on the big goals you want to achieve, and you work backwards to identify how to do that effectively. The Day One mentality allows you to act like you're still in start-up mode, so that you can grow aggressively, stay relevant, and continue to innovate.

Day One is also about avoiding complacency company-wide. For big brands who already have established cultures and can't easily turn the vehicle while it's moving at speed, the future focus really needs to be about overcoming the inertia that can settle in when people are not using Day One thinking. It's about getting people to stay engaged with the work, to keep up to date on new best practices and new developments in your industry. It comes down to being plugged in and making this channel a priority.

There's no shortage of content to absorb, in the form of media, blogs, podcasts and presentations from thought leaders; what is more challenging is to filter that information for what is useful and relevant for your particular organization, and then synthesize that with your strategy.

Amazon is constantly coming up with new tools,

updating their guidelines and best practices, and creating new opportunities for brands to test. This means that if your organization is complacent, or allows a 'set and forget' mentality, you will constantly be behind. You will get stuck chasing the platform and chasing your competitors.

It's key to go into your Amazon transformation being prepared to continually optimize your presence, proactively research new developments and trends, and always be on the lookout for new opportunities. Committing to test-and-learn strategies will help you stay on top of all this change in real time, and will create a fast-paced environment that innovates at the speed of Amazon.

Day One Vs Innovation (Or, Cash Today Vs Growth Tomorrow)

In Chapter 5 we mentioned another Amazon leadership principle, Invent and Simplify: *"Leaders expect and require innovation and invention from their teams and always find ways to simplify. They are externally aware, look for new ideas from everywhere, and are not limited by 'not invented here.' As we do new things, we accept that we may be misunderstood for long periods of time."*

There's a great deal of overlap between Day One thinking and nurturing a culture of innovation. They are two sides of the same coin and they fuel each other: Day One is focused on today, while innovation is focused on tomorrow. Innovation requires real foresight, but you don't get a return today from innovation—you get a return today by putting more dollars into your Sponsored Ad campaign. The timelines are completely different, so the C-suite has to prioritize innovation over the mid- to long-term, while also maintaining the momentum and returns of Day One thinking.

From a budget perspective, this can be a challenge. You know you can invest in proven strategies and get a specific return, but you know you also need allow budget to properly test and learn in areas where the organization needs to develop experience and knowledge.

Sometimes brands miss the mark on this—for example, a couple of years ago, some brands invested in the development of Alexa and voice search capabilities, but saw little reward for their efforts in the short-term. Because there was no immediate return, CFOs pulled the funding for development and the budget and resources were shifted elsewhere. Today, voice search is becoming critical—those companies were real innovators, but now they have to go back to the beginning, formulate the business case again, hire talent that are now more experienced (and more expensive), and rework their understanding of new best practices.

That's the balance with innovation. Sometimes you innovate too early, and end up having to pause your initiatives until the market is ready for them. This is why innovation needs foresight and commitment from the C-suite, because building the business case can be a challenge. A CFO might be reluctant to sign off on a test-and-learn budget from the CMO if there's no hard data or analysis to justify the plan and investment. That's why it's critical that all the executives are aligned on how the company will portion out investment into areas that will help future-proof their business.

To be clear, spending on innovation is not just about pouring money into complete 'unknowns' or barely-viable technologies that won't see the light of day for years to come. It's about spending a small percentage on a new tactic your organization hasn't tried before, on a new channel you're not experienced in, or technologies and platforms that are emerging in the market. It's about developing experience with the innovations that have the potential to scale, so that you can grow with them as they become powerful forces in the market.

This approach calms the fears of the CFO, because there's a much clearer path to a return on that investment in the short-term. Some of the budget allocated to innovation can go to new ad formats, or to testing a new pricing model, or creating a new experience or forging a new partnership. Let's say you do manage to get a 10% allocation here—that percentage can be split up further to ensure that you do start seeing returns quickly. Maybe 2% goes to testing ideas that are completely new and experimental, 5% goes to testing channels that look promising (but where the company needs firsthand experience), and the remaining 3% can go to strategies that are proven but haven't yet been implemented within your company. This is not about throwing 10% of your budget at ideas that might never generate any return.

Amazon is an ideal sandbox for innovation because they often invite leading brands to test initiatives that are truly at the cutting edge of retail technology. They launch new types of ad units regularly, test initiatives across sales, marketing, operations and fulfilment, and frequently trial new content experiences all over the ecosystem.

Monica Ferguson, CEO of Solemates, a company that makes foot and shoe care products, explains the incremental innovation they're experiencing with Amazon:

"Amazon is always throwing new things our way, and we've been happy to be guinea pigs for many things they've done. We've been on their Launchpad program, we've done lots of live streaming, where I get to stream direct to the Amazon community off my phone. It's pretty amazing, the reach you can get with these live streams, and you can promote them to broaden your audience too.

We go into all these things saying *"Yes, we'll try this out and see what the effect is on our customer experience."* Do we see more eyes on our product detail page? Are we seeing a higher click-through rate? If it's working, we'll continue to do it, and if it doesn't we can always decide that it's not for us.

We always say yes to any opportunity that comes our way with Amazon, and then opt out if it's not working out for us. Amazon wants people who want to be part of their new platforms and it's clear they know it needs to be a money-making enterprise for everyone too."

Innovation doesn't necessarily need to be a completely new invention or strategy; it can simply be a new channel or initiative for your brand. That's why Amazon can be categorized as an innovation strategy: many brands have not invested appropriately in the platform, so getting started is an innovation internally, even though Amazon has been around for 25 years. In the next sections, we explore

Amazon's future areas of innovation and how you can best capitalize on these opportunities.

Big Data

Whilst brands and marketers are already scaling Amazon's marketplace and advertising solutions, there will eventually be an opportunity to leverage Amazon's rich first-party retail and audience data sets far beyond what is currently possible. This is thanks to Amazon Web Services (AWS), which is a major, innovative division of Amazon's total business. AWS provides the technology infrastructure that powers a huge number of websites and Internet applications, and brands will have an incredible opportunity once they are able to compare their own first-party data and marketing metrics with all of Amazon's data.

The secret is out that Amazon is developing 'clean room' data technology with the aim of improving measurement and data comparison for ad campaigns. Similar in concept to Google's Ads Data Hub (ADH) or Facebook's enterprise data-sharing service, this is a measurement and analytics product. It will allow brands to mix their own advertising and retail data with partner data in an AWS environment, which will improve ad campaign performance and provide deeper insights into customer behavior.

Brands will need to prepare for this development and evaluate its potential. Many companies have already invested heavily in the deployment of a marketing cloud (like those provided by Adobe, Salesforce, Oracle and others), a DMP (Data Management Platform) and some are even launching the newer concept of a CPD (Customer Data Platform). These platforms are where brands store their first-party data, and where they can mix that with third-party or partner data to find the rich insights that might drive their business forward.

Some brands have struggled to corral the necessary resources for these platforms to deliver the promised results, and many CMOs have stated that they were oversold on the dream of what these platforms could deliver. Evaluating Amazon's new data offering might therefore be politically sensitive for CMOs and CTOs to navigate (particularly considering that returns may not yet have been realized from previous investments, and that any change in provider will come at an extra cost).

However, considering the wealth of data—and the ability to activate directly on those insights that Amazon's solution may facilitate—it may well be worth the additional investment. Data is the currency that modern retail runs on, and brands now have to consider their data infrastructure as a key part of their strategic decisions.

Voice Assistant Capabilities

Voice search is an early demonstration of the power that AI and Natural Language Processing (NLP) will bring to retail, enabling brands to create highly personalized consumer experiences in a completely new modality. Voice search (as we currently have with applications like Amazon Alexa and Google Assistant) is a forerunner to brands being able to communicate with customers directly—in their home, in their car, while they're out walking their dog. This advanced technology is being designed to understand who we are as individuals, to be able to interact with us in a human-like way, and to understand our personal methodology for navigating Amazon. This design intent will enable voice search to give us personalized content, product recommendations and experiences, both on and off the platform.

While Google plans to dominate personalized search, Amazon plans to dominate personalized commerce. Voice and all the AI-driven personalization technologies that are being developed are highly convenient mediums that are transforming customer behavior. The customer journey used to require people to get in their cars and go to the store. The next evolution meant consumers had to go to their computer. The next iteration had them to go to their smartphone, and now they can be anywhere—voice capability means that they don't have to change anything about what they are currently doing. Consumers can literally keep typing away at their emails, have a thought mid-sentence, and say, "Hey Alexa, order five Tide pens." The typing goes on uninterrupted and a purchase is executed instantly—the path to purchase has become a single action, rather than a long sequence of actions. The disruption and resistance that has always accompanied purchasing decisions has become virtually non-existent. This will eventually be completely seamless with voice-activated technology, and the AI is only going to keep getting better.

As NLP has finally caught up to current AI capabilities, voice has integrated very smoothly into the home, where many people make a lot of their purchasing decisions, do research, engage with entertainment and plan their lives. It's as frictionless as any marketer could dream of, and brands need to work out how they are going to establish a presence in voice search, in order to establish a presence in the consumer's home.

Again, there's a spectrum about how far into this innovation brands will go. For some companies it may make sense to invest heavily in this area, and for others, it may be more sensible to keep an eye on it while others take the lead (since this area is yet to mature and there is a lot of experimentation left to do).

For CPG and retail brands, if the ultimate goal is to have people discover your brand and buy your products, then the simplest first step is to get a handle on voice SEO. Just as we've all had to adapt to how each different tech platform's algorithms prioritize results, we'll soon start to see patterns and best practices emerge around voice SEO. How do people search for products and make purchases differently when they're using voice? How do they speak to Alexa compared to how they enter a search term into Google or Amazon?

Amazon has previously said that they won't run ads on voice search, but that seems unlikely to us. More probable is that they will find a way to monetize Alexa with minimal disruption to the customer experience, serving up sponsored results that brands will need to invest in to leverage. The advertising formats will likely be different to traditional radio formats, with less ad inventory available and at a higher premium. For example, serving a promotion to a specific customer might cost $1 on a sponsored ad campaign on desktop or mobile, but it might cost $5 through voice, and be served at a lower frequency.

Brands are going to have to familiarize themselves with a new set of economics for this new format. There are many technologies that are catching up and may start to scale—visual search, augmented search and so on—but they are unproven at this point and the use cases for brands haven't crystallized yet. However, voice assistants are here to stay and will present huge opportunities for brands, so it's key to keep an eye on what's developing in this space.

The B2B Marketplace

Another massive area of growth for Amazon is B2B. From a market size standpoint, B2B is double the size of the consumer market. Hospitals, offices, governments, schools, and militaries are buying everything from pencils to industrial equipment.

B2B has a well-established way of doing business, usually run by distributors and closed networks. Powerful intermediaries exist in B2B purchasing, and just as many stores are disappearing on the consumer side, B2B intermediaries are having their business model tested by e-commerce: Amazon also enables institutions to buy products directly from their supplier of choice, and to enjoy a much better purchasing experience. It can be surprising to some brands just how many orders come through from businesses, restaurants, offices and so on when they enrol their products on Amazon's business platform. People are buying all manner of things for their workplaces and Amazon is very well placed to take a huge share of those sales, because the same people are often buying from Amazon at home for their personal lives. They're familiar with the system and they're confident that Amazon will give them good service, so Amazon has a uniquely powerful position to meet the needs of the B2B market.

In the future, we might also see Amazon becoming a facilitator of trade between businesses, whether that's through payment processing, providing infrastructure, or connecting service providers. It's also likely to increase its search capabilities to other purchasing behaviors (such as going to restaurants, buying real-world experiences, or hiring tradespeople). This becomes much broader than product search, because Amazon has serious market penetration across verticals, and so much power in peoples' purchasing habits. Businesses will need to skill up to capitalize on these trends and to ensure they are capturing as much of the B2B opportunity as possible.

Omni-Channel Integration

Many brands are concerned about how they should integrate their existing retail channels with their e-commerce strategy, in order to create a consistent customer experience across both in-store and online interactions. Working with dozens of brands that are concerned with cross-channel cannibalization, we've rarely seen it happen to the extent that brands are concerned about. This is because an Amazon shopper (and particularly a Prime shopper) is generally very loyal, and is unlikely to seek out a brand or product on other channels if it is not available on Amazon.

The success of integrating your physical presence in stores with your e-commerce presence really depends on who owns the stores your products are in. If you're selling to Macy's, you probably know even less about your end customer than you know about your Amazon customers. The exception is where brands are fully vertically integrated, but even where brands do have their own stores, many are struggling to parse their e-commerce data effectively enough to improve their in-store experiences anyway. The concern about owning the customer relationship on Amazon is really moot unless all the channels are vertically integrated and e-commerce data is being used to create a specific connection with customers in stores.

In a *Forbes* article titled "Omni-channel Is Dead. The Future Is Harmonized Retail," retail commentator Steven Dennis says that it's time to accept the truth that "all the talk about different channels is not particularly helpful. The customer is the channel."[2] The customer has more choice than ever, so if they are choosing to be on Amazon, we need to do our best to serve them on Amazon. If they move to another platform, we need to do our best to serve them there. The customer is what we need to plan around, instead of planning exclusively around the channel itself.

NINE

NEXT STEPS

Amazon Leadership Principle:
Bias For Action

"Speed matters in business. Many decisions and actions are reversible and do not need extensive study. We value calculated risk taking."

———

IN THIS FINAL CHAPTER, we want to leave you with some practical steps for implementing the recommendations we have made in this book and to prepare your organization to thrive in the new Amazon economy. Most importantly, we're going to share our advice on how to choose and manage strategic partners that can help you develop and execute the right Amazon strategy for your brand.

Start With Strategists

As we've discussed, brands reap the most success with all the opportunities Amazon offers when they approach this giant platform with a holistic strategy. You can implement the strategy internally, engage agencies do it for you, have consultants advise you, or have software automate the tasks —but regardless of how you structure your approach, it's vital that your partners are able to collaborate and be transparent. Amazon touches so many parts of the business, from retail and e-commerce to warehousing and fulfilment, from product packaging to content and advertising, that if you do choose to bring in external partners, you also need an internal point person to bring all the different parties together and to keep the strategy moving forward cohesively.

In an interview with *Digiday*, Matt Meeker, CEO of dog supplies brand Bark, explained that the right approach for his company was to hire a small internal team of domain experts, and then to bring in an external consultant with Amazon experience to help the team engineer their strategy over the course of twelve months. The outcome of that partnership was both innovative and highly effective: "The idea was to reverse engineer our products to find out where the most opportunity for product development was, and then build the line out from there," said Meeker. Bark launched on Amazon with five products in mid-2018, and was projecting 10X growth by the end of 2019.[1]

To get the best outcome, then, it's important to choose partners who are open to a collaborative approach, who understand that they're not going to be specialists at every part of an Amazon strategy, and who are realistic about what they can handle (and where they, in turn, need to find partners to plug the gaps). Amazon is far too broad for anyone to have a handle on every single piece, so your agency partners and other providers need to be truly ready to collaborate with each other. They need to work together to put you as the client first, to align to your goals and mission for success, and to be willing to work with whichever parties are necessary to help achieve this.

One issue many brands run into here is that they already have an agency of record, or an agency handling performance marketing on other channels. Instead of researching and evaluating who the most appropriate partners might be, the brand goes to their agency of record to ask if they can also handle Amazon, and of course, the agency says yes. But just because you have a relationship with an agency, and they have been effective on other channels, there's no guarantee they're going to be great with Amazon. Like brands, some agencies are only just waking up to Amazon, and only the most progressive among them have fully built out their Amazon capabilities. So if you have an existing agency, make sure you ask some key questions before committing your Amazon channel to their care:

- Who is going to be responsible for your account?
- How much experience do they have with Amazon specifically?
- How does their approach differ for Amazon compared with other platforms?
- What Amazon-specific resources do they have at their disposal?

Because Amazon strategy and execution are still quite nascent skillsets within the traditional agency world, it's key to ensure they do have someone on board that really knows the platform, and ideally *only* handles the Amazon channel for clients.

It's also important to choose partners who are agile, who can respond quickly and effectively on short notice. It's ineffective to work with a company who comes out of a meeting and returns a solution to you two months later—you need real responsiveness, because Amazon works far too quickly for those kinds of delays. Agencies should be able to prove they can act fast, and you should feel confident giving them a mandate to do so. If just one partner in the chain can't deliver on this, it can scupper your entire strategy, so it's key that everyone is on board with this fast-paced approach. They must be comfortable with the pace of Amazon, with a culture of change and innovation, and clear that this responsiveness an important part of their role with you.

Bigger agencies making big claims about their Amazon capabilities should be vetted particularly for this—do they *really* move fast? What does 'fast' actually mean to them? Sometimes the best option is to have a mix of small, agile partners who can move with immediacy on the implementation and operational side, and a larger agency who can deliver the strategy and media scale at a slightly slower pace. In this case, each partner should be kept up to date on what the others are doing, so that you can avoid any potential conflicts or double-handling.

Regardless of how you choose to proceed, it's important (as always) to ensure there are regular moments to assess where everyone is at on the path to success, and for all parties to ensure they are aligned. Each time you bring your Amazon-related teams together, they should be able to contribute to the strategy and conversation in a meaningful way, cross-pollinating ideas and sharing insights. Regular meetings with partners will allow you all to constantly work backwards from the agreed goal and to identify what each party needs to be doing at any given time.

Regular partner meetings also mean that you can see when collaboration is faltering. Everyone says they are collaborative, but if you start to see teams going into protectionist mode, where important information or data is not being shared, it's very useful to have scheduled opportunities to get everything back on track. The siloed approach might have been tolerable when companies had a single agency of record handling everything for all their channels, but Amazon is a different beast and the only way to win is to work together. If different parties are focused on their own priorities, inefficiency creeps in, teams start to get frustrated, and problems start to arise.

For example, the strategy for your Amazon search campaigns—from a purely technical standpoint—is completely different to how you structure Google Adwords campaigns. Sharing the keywords that are performing best on Google Adwords can be helpful background for initiating Amazon campaigns, but if a team takes a shortcut and copies the Google campaigns straight into the Amazon advertising console, they just won't work. The same strategies simply do not apply to every channel, so there has to be collaboration about best practices and tactical implementation.

Fair attribution is another critical reason for collaboration. In both of our experience, when our clients run a campaign outside of Amazon that performs very well (which might include paid media campaigns on other channels, a huge push with PR, a social media campaign, influencer campaigns etc.), we see total sales on Amazon go up, *and* we see our own ads working better on Amazon. For example, consumers might see an ad on Facebook, open Amazon in a new browser tab, search for the product, see a consistent ad for the same brand on Amazon, then click on the Amazon ad and buy the product. Who should get the attribution for that?

In a traditional model, the Amazon advertising agency would get the attribution, even though the agency activating the Facebook campaign played the key part. This is obviously where the separation between the channels gets muddy, and it's why you need all your partners to know what everyone else is up to, so that you can see that any surge in traffic and conversions is accurately credited. In this example, if the agency is running a massive Facebook campaign and the Amazon agency hasn't contributed, the Facebook agency should get the attribution, and the client will be able to see what is really working. Although it's challenging to insist on collaboration between multiple agencies, when all your partners are talking to each other and seeking clarity on what's happening within each walled garden or channel, you can start accurately piecing together what's working. These increased insights are a major reason we're so focused on the importance of choosing collaborative service providers as early in your Amazon transformation as possible. Be mindful of preventing information-hoarding from creeping into your operation, and ensure that all your partners and internal teams are proactively building connections with each other to maximize all the different functions within your Amazon strategy.

Holding Partners Accountable

Keeping your partners accountable relies on developing real clarity on what your objective is on Amazon, and to be realistic about achieving that objective. It's not realistic to go to your agency and say, "We want to double our sales in the next two months, and we also want to cut our ad spend by 40%." Those objectives are totally at odds with each other, and your partner should challenge you if the goals presented are unrealistic. A good agency leader who knows that your primary objective is to be as profitable as possible on this channel is going to run a very different strategy to what they would run if your objective were to take over a category and aggressively acquire market share. Collaborate with your agency on what is realistic—experienced professionals will push back on unrealistic goals, and suggest more meaningful alternatives. But once an agency or partner has agreed to a strategy for your brand, they should become accountable for achieving it.

Charlie Cole, Chief Global E-Commerce Officer at Samsonite, and Chief Digital Officer at Tumi, shares his view on accountability:

 "If you have a really big agency and you're buying brand media, you have to appreciate that it's in your best interest to maintain the status quo—you don't necessarily want to have this next level of accountability and analytics that digital frankly guarantees. There's something to be said for fighting against the status quo in your organization and taking the initiative to hold brand media to a higher level than it has been before. When you have people who are unwilling to do that, it raises my hackles a little bit and makes my spidey sense tingle that there's something deeper going on. I think we should all strive for accountability, particularly in digital media."

Many big brands ask for efficiency on their media spend, which will likely influence how the Amazon strategies at those companies are developed. They may demand the cheapest rates they can get for their media spend, but this is really not how a biddable environment like Amazon operates, since demand drives prices up.

That said, Amazon is already cutting deals with big spenders, as Facebook and Google have done, and since agencies lead those deals, CMOs will rely on their agencies and their collective buying power to cut better rates on DSP fees and commitments on volume. As big agencies become more and more responsible for huge brand spend on Amazon in the future, they will wield more power, and this may go the same way as the old TV model—the lower the rates you can negotiate, the more attention you can buy.

A lot of agencies work on a percentage of total sales, so it's clearly in their best interest to grow revenue as much as possible. But this model can lead to poor short-term decisions and a focus on increasing media spend. Brands are used to paying a percentage of media spend or various other models, and will have different models of accountability for their agencies.

There's not going to be a one-size-fits-all model, but the performance of your agreed metrics of success are key indicators. When your media is performing well, it's obvious, because you see increases in conversions, repeat purchases and customer engagement.

If you plan to pay a partner based on performance (usually a percentage of sales, or incremental sales), be prepared for the potential disincentives that come with that model. In advertising, it's common for agencies to be compensated with a percentage of spend. That doesn't necessarily promote highly efficient campaigns or any interest in driving your costs down—it incentivizes the agency to spend as much money as possible without concern for efficiency. If you've got a growth-at-all-costs mentality, maybe that will work for you, but if you have a focus on profitability, or you have budget constraints, then that inefficiency can present a real downside.

Many smaller brands want to incentivize their agencies based on performance, as a percentage of topline sales or sales incremental to the current level. But there are disincentives there too, because the agency might push strategies that are shortsighted, such as getting reviews in a noncompliant way, or recklessly driving up ad spend.

And as we mentioned earlier, don't forget that what you do outside of Amazon has an impact on what happens inside of Amazon. In that topline compensation structure, you might ultimately reward your Amazon agency for campaigns that they were not involved with, so there needs to be consideration on the best model for compensation and plenty of transparency and accountability in your relationship with your partners.

The Mandate To Challenge

As part of cultivating transparency and accountability, it's powerful to give your partners a mandate to challenge you. For your Amazon presence to thrive, you need agency partners that are strategic, confident in their own knowledge and experience, and that can deliver. Once you have secured a partner, ensure you create a transparent relationship where challenges are encouraged and not punished.

Partners should be willing to challenge you on the brief, to challenge the strategy to ensure it's as robust as possible, and to challenge complacent thinking or short-term focus.

Some agencies just say yes to everything, and if you don't have a relationship where you can challenge each other, it becomes very difficult to test and learn, to innovate, and you really can't test the boundaries of what's possible. The agency is there to be the domain expert—they need to come to you with realistic suggestions and healthy expectations about what you can achieve together. You have to encourage debate and overcome the temptation to just see the agency as the execution team (though you should also be willing and able to challenge the agency right back, to ask questions and engage in robust dialog to ensure the best outcomes).

To be successful on Amazon you must be open to ideas, be willing to try new things, and empower the people you've chosen to drive your objectives forward. As agency leaders, we know that the best projects happen with clients who are committed, accessible, responsive, and empowered to make decisions. And when those clients respond quickly to innovative ideas, are willing to take some risks, and are excited to move fast to grasp an advantage, that's when the engagement can become truly transformative. Amazon is changing every day, so having partners you can ideate with and who are empowered will make for win-win projects.

Success on Amazon starts and ends with education. As we have already discussed, Amazon is not a one-and-done channel—its constant rate of change requires ongoing education and analysis. There are a few key strategies we recommend to meet this challenge:

1. Read news and analysis to keep up to date on changes on the platform. Your teams should also be held accountable to this ongoing research. There is a mass of content published about Amazon every week, and the insights from experts can provide practical, up-to-date information across the platform.

2. Join or create a peer group (either formally or informally). We all need associates and peers with whom we can ideate, stress-test ideas and share insights. The two of us do this together, often swapping notes on new programs and approaches ourselves. Ideally, you would also model this approach for your team—they will thrive when they have peers to learn from too.

3. Learn from your partners. If you take our advice here, you'll select partners who are collaborative, which means they should be willing (within reason) to help you advance your knowledge. This includes getting your hands dirty occasionally—it can be very valuable to sit down with your team or partners, explore the advertising console, familiarize yourself with the brand's vendor or seller account, and get a sense of how the tactical puzzle fits together on Amazon.

FINALLY, we want to reiterate just how important it is that the organization as a whole commits to the Amazon strategy you choose. Everyone involved needs total clarity about the goals for the channel, and what the path to success will look like. Relying heavily on the Amazon Leadership Principles is also critical—to thrive with Amazon, you have to think like Amazon. It might sound reductive, but it's true: the more your company can embrace the principles of customer obsession, diving deep, taking ownership, and embracing innovation, the greater the success you are likely to see on Amazon.

AS WE SAID right at the start, we wrote this book because we have skin in the game. We're practitioners in this field and we have businesses that help brands with their Amazon channels. We know that Amazon is only going to get bigger and more influential on consumer culture, and we want to see brands taking advantage of it.

At this stage you understand that you need a partner who is looking at Amazon holistically and understands all the different aspects it touches across a business. That partner needs to help audit where you are, formulate a strategy and vision, and then help you deliver a phased, agile approach to reach that success. That's the Amazon agency of the future—they're not just focused on sales and the marketplace, but they're also preparing for what's coming, with a clear sense of how vast and impactful the platform is and will continue to be.

Whether your brand is already up and running on Amazon, or you're just about to take a first step into this space, we want to help your brand to thrive. We'd love to hear from you about the unique challenges and opportunities you are facing with Amazon. We won't be the right fit for every company, but at the very least we'll be able to help you identify what you need, and point you in the direction that will help you start seeing real success on this incredible channel.

Mark's agency, Podean, specializes in strategic, holistic brand building on Amazon, coming to the platform with many years of media and upper funnel strategy experience. Kiri's agency, Bobsled, is focused on protecting brands, growing sales, running marketplace operations, and scaling with advertising.

And for brands that aren't ready to work with external partners, or that want to upskill their internal teams on this channel, The Marketplace Institute is a platform for brands and agencies to develop their Amazon capability, including a knowledge base of all the processes the Bobsled team uses to manage hundreds of Amazon accounts. It's what Bobsled account managers and specialists use day-to-day, and we're opening up our best practices to brands and other agencies who need to develop their skillsets in this area. It also includes the first ever 'Amazon Helpline'—on-demand access to subject matter experts who can help you troubleshoot and strategize in tricky situations.

The brands that thrive in the new Amazon economy are those that stay open, curious and willing to test new initiatives. They're agile, they're not stuck in the past and they're optimistic about the potential that technology and data are bringing to the retail world. If you've made it to this point, we suspect you're the embodiment of that attitude, and it's been our privilege to share our experience and knowledge with you. We hope this book has given you the insight and clarity needed to steer your company through its own Amazon transformation, and we wish you every success as you lead your organization into the future.

NOTES

Introduction

1. https://www.cbsnews.com/news/amazon-prime-day-more-than-half-of-american-households-will-be-amazon-prime-members-in-2019/
2. https://www.vox.com/2017/6/8/15759354/amazon-prime-low-income-discount-piper-jaffray-demographics
3. https://techcrunch.com/2018/07/13/amazons-share-of-the-us-e-commerce-market-is-now-49-or-5-of-all-retail-spend/
4. https://www.sec.gov/Archives/edgar/data/1018724/000119312517120198/d373368dex991.htm

1. Navigating The New Amazon Economy

1. 1 https://www.amazon.jobs/en/principles
2. https://www.linkedin.com/pulse/how-interview-amazon-leadership-david-anderson/
3. https://www.inc.com/brian-de-haaff/brilliant-ceos-do-not-obsess-over-competitors-n.html
4. https://www.forbes.com/sites/kirimasters/2018/08/21/shoppers-prefer-online-marketplaces-over-retailers-repeat-purchases/#42d5860279f4

3. Strategic Frameworks For Success

1. https://www.podean.com/amazon-explained-the-flywheel/
2. https://retailgeek.com/jason-scot-show-episode-125-jandj-sri-rajagopalan/
3. https://blog.aboutamazon.com/company-news/amazon-project-zero

4. The Two-Edged Sword: Threats & Challenges

1. https://digiday.com/retail/problem-pervasive-inside-popsockets-fight-amazon-fakes/
2. https://www.forbes.com/sites/kirimasters/2019/07/30/amazon-launches-its-first-b2b-private-label-brand/#23ca166d70eb

3. https://www.scrapehero.com/everything-you-need-to-know-about-amazon-private-labels/
4. https://retailgeek.com/jason-scot-show-episode-125-jandj-sri-rajagopalan/
5. https://www.marketplacepulse.com/articles/amazon-is-a-monopoly-an-interview-with-sally-hubbard
6. https://www.forbes.com/sites/kirimasters/2019/05/22/why-some-merchants-are-avoiding-amazon/#707b35f63172

5. Winning On Amazon: Outcomes & Goals

1. https://www.businessinsider.com/heres-the-surprising-way-amazon-decides-what-new-enterprise-products-to-work-on-next-2015-3
2. https://www.podean.com/amazon-explained-amazon-working-backward/
3. https://www.emarketer.com/content/us-advertisers-still-eager-to-target-at-scale-with-duopoly

6. Organizational Design In An Amazon World

1. https://digiday.com/retail/retail-briefing-how-one-cpg-brand-built-a-business-on-amazon/

8. Future Opportunities & Considerations

1. https://www.podean.com/amazon-explained-the-day-1-mentality/
2. https://www.forbes.com/sites/stevendennis/2019/06/03/omni-channel-is-dead-the-future-is-harmonized-retail/#67454f0c65e8

9. Next Steps

1. https://digiday.com/retail/retail-briefing-barkbox-beat-amazon-game/

ACKNOWLEDGMENTS

We would like to thank all the people who have helped develop us and mentor us over the years. Our employees, our partners and all our clients have made this book possible, and we're deeply grateful for the opportunities and insights we've been able to explore together. We also want to make a special note of thanks to all the business leaders who made so much of their time available to us and were so willing to share their experiences in order to enrich this material.

ABOUT THE AUTHORS

Kiri Masters

Kiri Masters is the founder and CEO of Bobsled Marketing, a digital agency created to help consumer product brands grow and protect their Amazon marketplace channels.

After a successful career as a commercial banker at JPMorgan Chase, Kiri launched her first e-commerce business on Amazon. Recognizing that the enormous potential of the channel would also require significant expertise, it wasn't long until Kiri decided to build a team of true Amazon experts to provide a platform for brands that are looking to grow.

Her entrepreneurial mind and passion for e-commerce allowed Kiri to become a strong voice for brands navigating online marketplaces. She is the author of *The Amazon Expansion Plan*, a more tactical guide to Amazon, and today is a contributor at *Forbes,* where she writes about Amazon from a brand's perspective, as well as hosting the E-Commerce Braintrust podcast.

In 2019, Kiri also founded The Marketplace Institute, an education platform for brands who are looking to develop their internal Amazon capabilities, upskill their team, and have the benefit of fast, phone-based access to legitimate expertise along the way—the first ever 'Amazon Helpline' for brands and agencies.

Kiri is married with a young child, who ensures she is not constantly thinking about Amazon.

Mark Power

Mark is a passionate and dynamic entrepreneur and business leader with diverse global experience across digital media, marketing technology and e-commerce.

He's the founder and CEO at Podean, the marketplace marketing experts. His team is building brands and driving growth across the entire Amazon ecosystem and emerging consumer marketplaces.

Previously, he was an executive at advertising holding company Interpublic (NYSE: IPG) as the Managing Director USA of the award-winning mobile and innovation agency Ansible. Recently Mark was Executive Vice President at Reprise, the digital performance media agency within IPG Mediabrands, where he led Growth and launched IPG's Amazon Center Of Excellence. In these roles he was fortunate to have partnered with brands such as Coca-Cola, BMW, Hulu, Johnson & Johnson, Spotify, Fiat Chrysler, Nationwide, Sony and Kia, driving the innovation and digital performance agendas.

Mark's personal passions are set solidly in the outdoors where he regularly competes in ultra-endurance running and cycling races around the globe, pushing his personal boundaries both mentally and physically. He also enjoys all winter and mountain sports and is incredibly passionate about his travels, exploring the world's oceans and rivers through pursuits such as sport fishing and diving. He is the father of two boys Hunter and Fisher, and husband to Vanessa. Mark and his family live in New York City.